Twayne's English Authors Series

Sylvia E. Bowman, *Editor*

INDIANA UNIVERSITY

John Middleton Murry

(TEAS) 72

John Middleton Murry

By ERNEST G. GRIFFIN

University of Alberta

Twayne Publishers, Inc.   : :   New York

To Marie

JOHN MIDDLETON MURRY

Preface

This study concentrates on John Middleton Murry's contribution to English literature. It does not concern itself with the many other facets of Murry's life and work except insofar as they appear helpful in illuminating his literary career. To learn more about Murry's extra-literary activities, the reader should consult the admirable biography by Mr. F. A. Lea.

At the same time, in any treatment of Murry's work, a wide interpretation must be allowed the phrase "contribution to literature." In spite of his great productivity—over fifty books and a vast number of essays, editorials, and reviews—Murry was essentially the amateur and non-specialist who would not acknowledge any serious distinction between life and literature. His life was most "undisciplined" in that he refused to separate it into the disciplines which, for example, are basic to the modern academic world. His personal associations, with Katherine Mansfield and D. H. Lawrence in particular, have become part of literary history; his books on religion and society drew their inspiration from his worship—the word is not too strong—of certain literary idols; and his active participation in the affairs of his time was the activity of a literary man molding the values by which, in his opinion, life and literature should be judged.

Even a brief statement of the extensive interests of Murry might suggest that he was not primarily a literary critic. But it is part of the enigma of Murry that he was just that—*primarily* a literary critic. Men of such divergent genius as T. S. Eliot and D. H. Lawrence have made a special note of this fact. His creativity went into criticism; and Herbert Read could observe that, at his best, he was the "most stimulating 'creative' critic" of his time. However far from literature "the experiencing self" (to use one of Murry's favorite terms) might roam, it existed only because it complemented the demands of another "self," the perceptive and evaluative critic.

The complex variety of Murry's work and experience has made the task of organizing this book a difficult one. Murry wrote on a great number of themes in the half-century of his writing life, returning to certain of them again and again over the years. Yet, viewed chronologically, his career manifests fairly distinct phases in thought and interests. There is, in the total pattern of his life, an interplay of idea and experience which, it is hoped, is reflected in this study. In brief, Chapter One deals with Murry's background and early attempts at different forms of writing and with the discovery of his true forte as literary critic; Chapter Two examines the formation of his critical premises, relating this to his long debate with T. S. Eliot; Chapter Three is concerned with his most significant period as critical essayist; Chapters Four and Five discuss the fundamental and all-pervading influence of Keats and Shakespeare and Murry's understanding of the English tradition in cultural life; Chapter Six explores his relationship with D. H. Lawrence and his lifelong attempt to come to terms with Lawrence's genius; and Chapter Seven deals with his final period and his return to criticism which was specifically literary.

I have been fortunate in receiving much kind help with this study. First, I must thank Mrs. Middleton Murry and Miss Ruth Baker, Mr. Murry's former secretary, for their generous assistance in answering questions and giving information. Not the least of the rewards in preparing this book has been the pleasure my wife and I have had in visiting the delightful cottage in Norfolk and enjoying their hospitality and friendship. Two friends of the late Mr. Murry have been particularly helpful in allowing me to quote from their own studies of Murry's life and work, namely Mr. F. A. Lea, who wrote the authorized biography, and Sir Richard Rees, who has edited one collection of Murry's essays and is now editing another. Of my academic colleagues, I want to give special thanks to Professor Dorothy Brewster of Columbia University for suggesting the book and keeping a kindly and watchful eye on its progress. Professor Henry Kreisel of the University of Alberta was kind enough to read the manuscript and offer valuable advice on points of fact and style. Like many other authors, I am very grateful to Professor Sylvia Bowman, Editor of the Twayne English Authors Series, for her expert and painstaking editorial work on the book. Finally, I am glad to take this opportunity of thanking The Canada Council for two grants enabling me to go to England for purposes of research.

ERNEST G. GRIFFIN

The University of Alberta

JOHN MIDDLETON MURRY

by

ERNEST G. GRIFFIN

At the present time, John Middleton Murry is perhaps best known as the husband of Katherine Mansfield and as the intimate friend, for a few years, of D.H. Lawrence. Many people, too, recall that he was satirised by Aldous Huxley in *Point Counter Point*. Unfortunately these aspects of Murry's reputation have overshadowed his very significant contribution to English literature and culture.

In the first place, he was a brilliant literary "talent scout" and critic. Herbert Read has observed that, at his best, Murry was the "most stimulating 'creative' critic" of his time. Many writers, now famous, have to thank him for his early recognition of their talents and for his influential critical support. As his work for *The Athenaeum* and the immensely successful *Adelphi* magazine demonstrates, he was one of his country's outstanding editors.

Apart from important books on Lawrence, Dostoevsky, Blake, Keats, Shakespeare and Swift, Murry wrote stimulating theoretical essays on metaphor and style and reintroduced to his readers some of the less famous treasures of English literature. At the same time he never lost interest in the contemporary intellectual scene; for example, he maintained an important literary friendship, and running debate, with T.S. Eliot.

An intriguing—if sometimes exasperating —mixture of critical Hellenism and Christian mysticism, Middleton Murry has an undeniably important place in the cultural history of England during the first half of the twentieth century.

Acknowledgments

Permission to include excerpts from John Middleton Murry's work has been granted by the Executors of the Estate of the late John Middleton Murry and by the Society of Authors as the literary representative of the estate. The author wishes to thank all those concerned in granting this permission, and also to thank the following firms for permissions to quote from Middleton Murry's books as indicated:

Jonathan Cape Ltd.: *To the Unknown God* (1924), *The Life of Jesus* (1926), *Love, Freedom and Society* (1957).

William Collins Sons and Co. Ltd.: *Aspects of Literature* (1920), *Countries of the Mind* (1922), *Discoveries* (1924).

Constable and Co. Ltd.: *Still Life* (1916), *The Things We Are* (1922).

Oxford University Press: *The Problem of Style* (1922), *Keats and Shakespeare* (1925).

Martin Secker and Warburg Ltd.: *Fyodor Dostoevsky: A Critical Study* (1916).

In addition, thanks are due to Methuen and Co. Ltd. for permission to quote from *The Life of John Middleton Murry* by F. A. Lea.

From THE COLLECTED LETTERS OF D. H. LAWRENCE, edited by Harry T. Moore. Copyright 1932 by the Estate of D. H. Lawrence, copyright © renewed 1960 by Angelo Ravagli and C. Montague Weekley, Executors of the Estate of Frieda Lawrence Ravagli. Reprinted by permission of The Viking Press, Inc.

Contents

Chronology

1889   John Middleton Murry born, August 6, in Peckham, London.

1901   Enters Christ's Hospital after winning scholarship. Good scholar, earning at sixteen the Charles Lamb Medal for an essay on "Literature and Journalism" and at eighteen the Gold Medal for Classics.

1908   Accepted at Brasenose College, Oxford, as result of scholarship. Continues studies in Classics.

1910–   Visits Paris. Greatly influenced by Post-Impressionism.
1911

1911–   Edits *Rhythm*. In 1911 meets Katherine Mansfield and
1913   begins career in journalism. Reviewer, then art critic, for *The Westminster Gazette*. In 1913, *Rhythm* becomes *The Blue Review*, which Murry edits with Katherine Mansfield for a few months before it ceases publication.

1913   Meets D. H. Lawrence. Close association between Murry, Katherine Mansfield, Lawrence, and Frieda until the summer of 1916, when it was virtually ended through disagreement. Some months later, Murry accepts position as translator at the War Office, London; becomes Chief Censor in 1918.

1916   Publication of *Fyodor Dostoevsky: A Critical Study*, his first long critical work, and *Still Life*, his first novel.

1917   Contributes regularly to *The Nation* and reviews French books for *The Times Literary Supplement*.

1918   Marries Katherine Mansfield, who dies at Fontainebleau of consumption in 1923. Subsequently edits the *Journal of Katherine Mansfield* (1927), *The Letters of Katherine Mansfield* (1928), *The Scrapbook of Katherine Mansfield* (1939), *Katherine Mansfield's Letters to John Middleton Murry, 1913-1922* (1951).

1919   Appointed editor of *The Athenaeum,* which closes in 1921. Publication of *The Critic in Judgment or Belshazzar of Barons Court,* a verse drama.

1920   Receives Order of the British Empire in recognition of his services during the War. Publication of *Cinnamon and Angelica,* a verse drama; *The Evolution of an Intellectual,* essays; and *Aspects of Literature,* essays.

1921   *Poems 1916—1920.*

1922   Publication of *The Problem of Style,* six lectures given at Oxford at the invitation of Sir Walter Raleigh; *Countries of the Mind: Essays in Literary Criticism;* and *The Things We Are,* a novel.

1923   Following the death of Katherine Mansfield, he has a decisive mystical experience which sets his "mind upon a chain of thinking which I have never relinquished." Edits, with great success, a new magazine, *The Adelphi.* Association with this magazine continues until 1948. Publication of *Pencillings: Little Essays on Literature.*

1924   Marries Violet le Maistre, who dies of consumption in 1931, leaving him a son and a daughter. Publication of *The Voyage,* a novel; *To the Unknown God,* essays; and *Discoveries,* essays.

1925   *Keats and Shakespeare: A Study of Keats' Poetic Life from 1816 to 1820.*

1926   *The Life of Jesus.*

1928   *Things to Come,* essays.

1929   *God: An Introduction to the Science of Metabiology.*

1930   *Studies in Keats.* This was to be revised over the years, becoming *Studies in Keats: New and Old* (1939), *The Mystery of Keats* (1949), *Keats* (1955).

1931   Marries Betty Cockbayne, who bears him a son and a daughter; marriage ends with her death in 1954. Liverpool University awards him the William Noble Fellowship for a study of Blake and Keats. Joins the Independent Labour Party, from which he resigns in 1934. Publication of *Countries of the Mind: Second Series,* essays; and *Son of Woman: The Story of D. H. Lawrence.*

1932   *The Necessity of Communism* and *The Fallacy of Economics.*

1933   *The Life of Katherine Mansfield* (with R. E. Mantz); *Reminiscences of D. H. Lawrence;* and *William Blake.* Twelve issues of *The Wanderer,* a small magazine written and published privately by Murry, appeared in 1933–34.

1935   Instrumental in founding *The Adelphi Centre* for promotion of a Socialistic society. Publication of *Between Two Worlds,* autobiography until the end of World War I.

1936   Converted to pacifism, joins the Peace Pledge Union. Through this association, meets Mary Gamble (1938). Becomes editor of *Peace News* (1940). Purchases Lodge Farm, Thelnetham, Norfolk, for experiment in community living (1942). In 1946 resigns from Peace Pledge Union and editorship of *Peace News,* renouncing his pacifism shortly afterwards. Publishes *Shakespeare,* an important critical work.

1937   *The Necessity of Pacifism.*

1938   Enters hospital; Bürger's disease diagnosed. *The Pledge of Peace* and *Heaven—and Earth,* a volume of essays, its American title being *Heroes of Thought.*

1939   *The Defence of Democracy; The Price of Leadership.*

1940   *The Betrayal of Christ by the Churches.*

1942   *Christocracy; The Dilemma of Christianity.*

1944   *Adam and Eve: An Essay Towards a New and Better Society.*

1948   *The Free Society; Looking Before and After*, essays; *The Challenge of Schweitzer*.

1949   *Katherine Mansfield and Other Literary Portraits*.

1950   *John Clare and Other Studies*.

1951   *The Conquest of Death*, a translation of Benjamin Constant's "Adolphe," followed by a long critical essay.

1952   *Community Farm*, the story of the experimental community and Lodge Farm.

1954   Marries Mary Gamble. Murry is by now a successful gentleman-farmer. Publishes *Jonathan Swift: A Critical Biography*.

1956   *Unprofessional Essays*.

1957   *Love, Freedom and Society*. Dies from heart attack. Buried in Thelnetham churchyard.

1959   Posthumous publication of *Katherine Mansfield and Other Literary Studies* and *Not as the Scribes: Lay Sermons*.

John Middleton Murry

CHAPTER 1

The Evolution of an Intellectual

"THERE are few harder fates for a man of some genius than to be intimately associated with a man of more. He is remembered, but in such a way that it seems better to be forgotten."[1] These words open an essay on William Godwin, but they could apply with equal truth to the author of it, John Middleton Murry. A friend of D. H. Lawrence and the husband of Katherine Mansfield, Murry has not only been underestimated for his own contribution to literature, but has been adversely, even bitterly, criticized for not being the friend or the husband he should have been. No one—as Murry continues in his comment on Godwin—"troubles to ask why it was that the man of greater genius found the intimacy of the man of smaller genius indispensable to himself."[2]

The quality in Murry which appealed to Lawrence is hard to define, but it had something to do with the uniqueness of his critical powers. Murry possessed a great gift of literary sensitivity; he was able, to an astonishing degree, to recognize what was of genuine literary value in a wide range of English and Continental literature. In the introduction to a posthumously published collection of Murry's essays, T. S. Eliot distinguishes between his own criticism, written mainly to aid the creative work of the artist, and Murry's: "Middleton Murry, on the other hand, was a literary critic first and foremost. . . . His originality—and he had indeed an original mind— went into his criticism."[3] In the same introduction, Eliot recalls an incident which illustrates the catholic and sure taste of Murry. For several years, Murry undertook the editorship of *The Athenaeum,* a post he filled with great distinction. On the basis of a first slender book of poems, Eliot was invited by Murry, who had not previously met the poet, to be an associate editor.

Murry dedicated himself not so much to his own writing as to the discovery of great writing, which, by definition, was writing done by great men. In this respect, he was a born disciple—a man, as he said, who had to have his heroes. Such heroes were never literary in a narrow sense. Like Homer for the early Greeks, they were educators and guides to living. In an early essay on Dostoevsky, Murry expressed the view that "an artist, great or small, works for the salvation of his own soul above all other things. If he works for other things he is a journeyman and a hireling."[4] Such a view of the artist's function directs the function of the critic. He was fond of quoting the remarks of his idol, Keats, not only that this world is a "vale of soul-making," but also that "we never really understand fine things until we have gone the same steps as the author." Murry tried to follow in the steps of the masters, and to encourage others to do so, not merely in order to imitate the masters—this would lead to the mediocrity which he did much to combat—but in order to share in the "soul-making" and in the artistic vision of the good life. His most important work—on Shakespeare, Keats, Blake, and Lawrence—follows this pattern.

There are many dangers in such an approach, and Murry did not avoid all of them. There is the obvious danger of *using* writers to solve one's problems, to the neglect of the literature. Murry was accused of this egocentric form of criticism, but, in general, both his theory and practice were beyond such naïveté. A more serious objection is that, because of his vast expectations of literature, he paradoxically gave up literary criticism in order to write books on—and take part in—religious and social affairs. His basic purpose, the search for permanent values, remained the same. But the sensitive and intuitive approach, which, balanced by standards derived from his Classical training, served him well in the criticism and editing of literature, led him to a disconcerting career in public life. He tended to discover the "permanent values" too quickly —in "the necessity of communism," in "the necessity of pacifism," in a defensive war against Russia, and so on.

But, when all the criticisms of him are made, the fact remains that he kept the great seriousness of literature. Although his type of criticism is not fashionable today, some of his books and essays are extremely good by any standards. He at times claimed that professionally he was a journalist. Perhaps he was the last of a great tradition which includes Hazlitt, De Quincey, and Sainte-Beuve (all influences upon him). He was the enlightened professional critic, the journalist who can reach his public and keep literature alive as part of the fullness of common life. He was not a "specialist" in the modern sense, but rather a "general critic." His concern was with "the general truths" of our culture and literary tradition, the larger significance of writers of the stature of Shakespeare, Keats, Blake, Dostoevsky, and Lawrence. No doubt such an all-inclusive attitude is out of keeping with the present age of analysis, and certainly it is easy to find looseness of statement in Murry's work. Yet the general critic who not only reminds us of the *topoi* of our culture but also tries to maintain the living quality in them, performs a necessary function. Like Matthew Arnold, whom he greatly admired, he had a Classic sense that life should be seen—and felt—as an ordered and harmonious whole:

The final purpose of literature remains "to see life steadily and see it whole"; but the definition is insufficient because it may equally be applied to the scientist or philosopher. The writer sees and recreates the quality of life as a whole, the quality of experience being precisely the element which is ignored by philosophy and science. Only in so far as the extension of the sensibility which comes with an advance in knowledge is made to heighten the perception of the quality of experience as a whole can it have a positive literary value.[5]

I Biographical Background

John Middleton Murry was born on August 6, 1889, in Peckham in the Borough of Camberwell, South London. His father was an ill-paid civil servant in the lower grades, who, like many in the same situation, desired his son to follow in his footsteps in the English government service, only on a higher level. As the father's income increased a little, the family moved slightly up the social ladder by moving from Peckham to the nearby but rather more genteel neighborhood of East

Dulwich. Naturally bright, Murry was encouraged by his parents to study for a scholarship: "The only moral imperative I knew in my youth was: 'Thou shalt work.' "[6] And he received it, one of the first scholarships to Christ's Hospital, which he entered, symbolically, at the very beginning of a new century in January 1901. He did well, receiving the Charles Lamb Medal for an essay on "Literature and Journalism" and, at eighteen, the Gold Medal for Classics.

Murry's sound Classical education at Christ's Hospital and later at Brasenose College, Oxford, was a most important factor in his intellectual attitude; for it had the effect of balancing journalistic haste and direct impressionism. But perhaps of equal importance for his future development was the feeling that accompanied his élite English Classical training of becoming "unclassed." The world of the majority of boys at Christ's Hospital was far different from that of East Dulwich; the differences ranged from the more obvious aspects, such as manners and speech, to deeper reverberations of thought and imagination. The terrors that young Murry endured when one of his relatives became too friendly with a school servant may seem reprehensibly snobbish when seen from a distance, but they were pangs which echoed a much deeper schism.

The boy Murry felt acutely the social and psychological gap which developed between himself and his home, between his own developing vision and the lower middle-class hopes of his family. Murry's long adventure in life to discover how and where to "belong" owes much to his early feelings of being "unclassed"—an early personal experience of what has become an increasingly important theme in contemporary British literature. Murry himself came to recognise the profound effect of this boyhood dislocation; fifty years later, in *Adam and Eve,* he described this breaking of the traditional social and educational pattern and the life-long effort to identify himself: "But the pattern was broken: and I did not make sense. As it were in my bones I came to feel during my time at Oxford that I did not make sense. And my life since then has been largely spent in an effort to make sense of myself."[7]

At Oxford he studied Classics under a generous and liberal-minded tutor, but he was not a dedicated scholar. His interests

were too widespread. A man who lived and learned by experience, he absorbed that offered by Oxford and was ready
for other experiences. His vacations in fact began to play a
larger part in his development than term time. Finding his
home now too suburban and tedious for him, he spent two
blissful vacations on a farm. In this novel, agricultural setting
he found a satisfaction which was fundamental. The farming
family of old yeoman descent became a firm center in Murry's
attitude to life, helping to give a pattern to his otherwise
surprising *volte-faces*. The farmer, Peachey, is described as
Thornhill in *Between Two Worlds* and as Williams in *The
Things We Are* with a Wordsworthian feeling of awe:

A nobler, more generous, warmer-hearted Englishman never trod the
earth than he.... Is there a manlier job in all the world than farming, a job that gives a man a juster pride or implants in him a truer
humility? At least, I never talked with John Thornhill on anything,
but I found myself talking more truly, more "in the middle of the
note" than I should otherwise have done.... Shakespeare and John
Thornhill—they are England to me—"the heart of generosity."[8]

. . . . .

Mr. Williams drove him to Luton. He enjoyed himself with the big,
solid man in the dog-cart. Everything about him was admirable....
He felt that Williams, with his puckered eyes, his untidy black mous-
tache, his weathered red skin, was a complete man.[9]

It is not surprising that Murry ended his life as a gentleman
farmer and that many years after the above was written he
used the image of the stout English oak to reveal his feelings
about the urban intelligentsia: around "the great oak of the
free society of Britain" is the "parasitic" ivy of "intellectuals
who are at work to confuse the moral sense of the British
people."[10]

Although Murry was constantly having ideas about new forms
of life and society, he did not—much to the distress of his followers—dedicate himself for long to any one of them. He
was not the prophet, like D. H. Lawrence, who lived a "new
consciousness" in an ever-developing vision. Murry frequently
expressed the need for a "new consciousness," but he apparently
worked best when tied—either in fact or by desire—to a tradi-

tion. From the security of the traditional he could experiment and criticize, often with great insight and shrewdness, but without the essential singleness of purpose which characterizes complete dedication to a new way of life. He may have been expressing a sense of this characteristic when he wrote: "By some chance or other I have always been quite incapable of the will to believe."[11]

While at Oxford, he seemed to be settling into the pattern of a cultured country life—doing well at the university and becoming engaged to the vicar's niece—when he was persuaded by Maurice Larrouy, a French literary man, to leave it all and go to Paris. In Paris, Murry was affected both by radical ideas (though in esthetic rather than social thought) and by a love affair with a French girl, Marguéritte, used as a theme in the first of his three novels, *Still Life*. As with his first engagement, he ended the affair by disappearing; but the shame of his desertion lasted a long time. The exciting new ideas he encountered were, in particular, those of Bergson and the Post-Impressionists; they in turn led to his first venture in a long and distinguished career as editor, of the magazine *Rhythm*, which lasted from the summer of 1911 to the spring of 1913 (lasting three months longer as *The Blue Review*).

Reading through these early fruits of his editorial ability, one is struck by the energy and manifesto-like statements, sometimes of rhapsodic tautology—"philosophy is the greatest art because art is the greatest philosophy"—and sometimes (as Murry was, in later times, the first to admit) grandly wrong— "Frank Harris is the greatest man and the greatest artist living among the English-speaking people ... the greatest writer of short stories that England has ever possessed ... the greatest creative critic whom the world has known." But, in spite of such vagaries, one can see developing the principles which were to remain fundamental to Murry as critic. The magazines also express the spirit that Murry never lost, that art is "a splendid adventure." Most of all, they reveal a critical sense of honor, which must be allowed Murry whatever one thinks of his ideas or actions: he was always ready to recognize the genuine search for truth and to give praise, even obeisance, to those who sought it.

One result of *Rhythm* was his meeting with Katherine Mansfield, several of whose stories were submitted to him as editor. A short time later the two met D. H. Lawrence and his wife-to-be, Frieda. This association has been much discussed and certainly has its place in the literary history of the twentieth century.[12] One immediate effect was that, through the persuasion of Katherine Mansfield, Murry left Oxford to work at journalism and reviewing for *The Westminster Gazette*.

During World War I, both Murry and Lawrence were excused military service on medical grounds, though Murry eventually accepted a post as translator in the War Office, rising to the position of chief censor and receiving the Order of the British Empire. During this period, with that remarkable ability to produce under all circumstances, Murry not only continued with his criticism and editing but also tried his hand at more "creative" work—poems, short stories, and (by 1924) three novels and two plays. It was, however, soon evident that his real talent lay in criticism. In 1916 he produced his first important book, *Fyodor Dostoevsky: A Critical Study,* setting the critical pattern for his later work on Keats and Shakespeare. His reputation was established by his editing of *The Athenaeum,* even though his editorship came to an end in 1921 with the merging of *The Athenaeum* with *The Nation.* Two years later Murry edited a new magazine, *The Adelphi,* the first issue of which was so successful that it had to be reprinted three times within two weeks. It continued to sell well; Murry had the knack of finding and appealing to the cultured public. Even when critics opposed his books, his public would buy them.

In the same year that *The Adelphi* began its career, an event occurred which Murry has designated as the most decisive of his life. After Katherine Mansfield's death in January 1923, he was in the depth of misery and overcome by a sense of loneliness that he longed to escape. He retreated to a remote cottage in Sussex to try to face the reality of his loneliness:

Slowly and with an effort I made myself conscious that I was physically alone. Prompted by some instinct I tried to force this consciousness into every part of my body. Slowly I succeeded. At last I had the sensation that I *was* in my hands and feet, that where they

ended I also ended, as at a frontier of my being, and beyond that
frontier stretched out vast immensities, of space, of the universe, of the
illimitable something that was other than I. Where I ended, it began
—other, strange, terrible, menacing. It did not know me, would never
acknowledge me, denied me utterly. Yet out upon this from the fragile
rampart of my own body, I found the courage to peer, to glance, at
last to gaze steadily. And I became aware of myself as a little island
against whose slender shores a cold, dark, boundless ocean lapped de-
vouring. Somehow in that moment I knew that I had reached a pin-
nacle of personal being. I was I, as I had never been before—and
never should be again.[13]

It was a moment of resurrection, in which darkness "changed
to light, the cold to warmth." The sense of loneliness was
replaced by a presence and a knowledge of belonging: "in
some way for which I had sought in vain so many years, I
belonged, and because I belonged I was no longer I." The
fear and menace disappeared; not only was Murry restored to a
sense of purpose, but the experience set his "mind upon a
chain of thinking which I have never relinquished." In de-
scribing the incident in God, he goes so far as to state: "Most
of what I have thought or written since that night and this
book itself have had their origin in the attempt to separate
the truth and value of that experience from whatever elements
of illusion, or potential illusion, it might contain."

There were, nevertheless, other important influences on his
thought. As several critics have pointed out, there seems to be
a definite link between Murry's marital career and the progress
of his ideas. This is not surprising when, as he said toward
the end of his life, quoting from one of his early poems, "Lo! I
have made love all my religion." "Love," in its widest sense,
was vitally connected with the "man-woman relationship"; and
Murry believed that this basic relationship did, and should,
affect the rest of a man's life. After the death of Katherine
Mansfield, history repeated itself in that it was through a magazine, The Adelphi, that Murry met his second wife, Violet le
Maistre, whom he married in 1924. It was, unhappily, a short
marriage, plagued by illness; and it ended in Violet's death in
1931 from consumption. And, as these facts indicate, there
is more than a suggestion that Violet had stepped into Kath-

erine Mansfield's shoes. In his next marriage, he turned away from the artistic and consumptive to the extrovert and gaily healthy Betty Cockbayne, the children's nurse; but this union proved to be a sad mistake, leading to conflict and final separation. Fortunately, he found the domestic happiness he had been seeking in his final marriage, to Mary Gamble, which became possible with the death of Betty in 1954.

Commenting on the relation of these marriages to Murry's changes in viewpoint, Mr. Lea writes: "Had he not made his marriage the touchstone of his faith? It was not by chance that, when hardening his heart against his wife [Betty], he had advocated anti-Fascist war; when aiming at her conversion, he had all but taken Orders; and when trying to reconcile her to Mary, he had preached a negotiated peace."[14] But a reviewer of Mr. Lea's book goes farther in summing up the wife-thought relationship: "With Katherine Mansfield he was literary; with Violet le Maistre ... metaphysical; with Betty Cockbayne (a good cook but a poor scholar) socialist and, under the stress of reconciling the irreconcilable, pacifist; with Mary Gamble, who provided him for the first time with the married bliss he craved, he was to become—bucolic."[15]

Although this last summary is, to say the least, too simple, Murry is open to the charge that he used his public life to compensate for the emotions and trials of private life. On another level, Murry could claim that he was following his deeper philosophy of living and learning by experience; and that, if others wished to learn from him, they could best do so by living *their* lives from the depth of feeling and experience. The ultimate gain would be a fullness and understanding of life, even in social communion, which could be obtained in no other way.

Although the progress of Murry's ideas between the wars and following World War II will be studied in succeeding chapters, in general his interests developed from the specifically literary to the religious and political. During World War II he was a pacifist and the editor of *Peace News*, but he renounced his pacifism after the war, even suggesting a defensive war against Russia. In 1952 he published *Community Farm*, the story of his attempt to create a new social organism based on the land—a happy chronicle which, with *The Free Society* and *Adam and Eve,* was the final working out of his social philosophy. He had become a gentleman farmer in Norfolk, completing, perhaps, the journey he had begun during the exciting holidays on a farm in his Oxford days when he had idealized the old English yeoman farmer.

During the final years of his life he returned increasingly to specifically literary criticism, this time without the constant pressure of a need for money. He died of angina pectoris in 1957.

II *Early Experiments*

Murry's efforts at "creative" work—poems, stories, novels, and plays—were not very successful; the analytic insight which sharpened his criticism seemed to act negatively when he tried to invent. Reading his poetry, one feels that the critic is never far distant. His lyrical poetry, often romantic, wistful, and elegiac, lacks the immediate simplicity which such poetry requires. There is not the right sense of easy pause and harmony —and the reader is bothered. The ideas and metaphors clatter together awkwardly. Occasionally, however, his intellectual awareness achieves a form of paradox reminiscent of metaphysical poetry: "Heart that believed yet shrunk, and shrinking half believed."[16]

His talent, it might be thought, was much better suited to the novel: a sense of place and character shows through in the autobiography, and D. H. Lawrence seems to have thought well at first of his attempts with the novel. But he was unable to expand his themes into fuller significance in his three novels: *Still Life* (1916), *The Things We Are* (1922), and *The Voyage* (1924). Bearing in mind the kind of biographical criticism he specialized in, one wonders why they are not successful. He was able to organize—certainly *The Voyage* has a well-planned form—and he was able to write good descriptive passages of life in London, from the chatter of literati to the quietness of introspective walking around in the rain. The quotations are given at some length because they serve also to give a picture of the milieu of the young Murry:

"Oh, you're too deep,"—Mrs. Fortescue had immediately conceived a dislike for him for his suggested opposition, and was trying to cover her aversion by playfulness. "I never think about things,—at any rate, not in that way. I mean that I never took any interest in pictures before these modern artists began to do these things. Now I'm absorbed. Besides I know quite a lot of them. They are so interesting when they tell you about their ideas; it gives you a feeling that you are mixed up in what is being done."

"Yes . . . I suppose it does. . . . I don't know very much about it. But what are their ideas?" Maurice felt that he would enjoy being hated by her for trying to make her ridiculous to herself. "I'm really interested."

"Oh, colour." She halted a minute, then ran smoothly into a remembered phrase. "The World is self-conscious and afraid of its own impulses. Modern art is the outcome of a desire to bring back colour as a source of pleasure in itself."

"Oh, a return to the savages."

"Exactly." She was secure now, having received her cue. "It is ridiculous to imagine we are superior to savages in everything. We're effete. The only thing to do is to go back to the primitive, uncontrolled people. They're splendid, unconscious. . . ."

Maurice wanted to continue; but suddenly he had a vision of himself and Mrs. Fortescue, Cradock and Mr. Fortescue, arranged mathematically at the corners of a square, one diagonal for the combatants, the other for the spectators. It was absurd.

"Well, it doesn't go well with the furniture," said Mr. Fortescue.[17]

Mr. Boston worked at Cadogan Square from 10 a.m. to 6 p.m. On Saturdays he went away at two o'clock. He had done this for four years now, with the exception of the week's holiday at Christmas and the fortnight in the summer for which he had originally stipulated; and he saw no reason why it should not go on for forty years. In the evenings he read, or wandered interminably in the London streets. He was accosted by women, he watched street fights, he sat in the remote seats of cinemas, drank at coffee-stalls, saw women sleeping in midwinter on the Embankment, women fighting each other amid a crowd of cheering men in Seven Dials, stared over bridges at the filthy yet regal Thames, listened to men preaching exasperated atheism in the Park, wondered at piercing solitary cries in the night. It was a sharp and jagged world, irremediably alien to him. He liked London best when a heavy rain was falling. The sudden sprouting of innumerable umbrellas, the sharp scream of the cab-whistles, the policemen standing unperturbed in their gleaming waterproofs, the soft sound of hurrying footsteps, the eager rush of water in the gurgling gutters, the bright shining of the wet roadways, the touch of the drops on his own face, comforted and thrilled him; he felt in these moments that he became a member of the great city.[18]

Unfortunately, such passages do not expand into a larger meaning. The reader, indeed, becomes impatient with the frivolously intellectual parties and with the hero who, after much heart-searching and discussion of love, somehow misses the full experience. In *The Voyage* the hero, Wickham, worries his way through his experience with three women: Anne, the girl who loves him; Mrs. Tancred, the married woman who plays with his feelings; and a prostitute. By a misunderstanding, which is something of a trick, he loses both Anne and Mrs. Tancred before any intimate liaison can occur. He walks as far as the door with the prostitute but leaves her there, though he pays the required amount. The novel is weak, not because of the hero's constant frustrations, but because Murry does not succeed in resolving esthetically the theme of dissatisfaction. D. H. Lawrence develops scenes of frustration until the reader feels he has reached a new level of understanding, but in Murry's novels the situation remains solidly static. There is rarely more than an egocentric fretting of the main character, a turmoil of feelings which subside without developing a sense of tragedy or comedy. Lawrence, who complained about such "self-indulgent melancholics," urged Murry to recognize that he was not inventive—"You must stick to criticism."[19] Murry was essentially one who *appreciated* his experiences; for all his intellectual wanderings, he was more conservative than inventive—a "conservative Romantic."

It is in his two plays that Murry's particular personal vision is given greater scope. The first, written in 1919, is *The Critic in Judgment or Belshazzar of Barons Court* in which he questions the critic's usefulness. The play begins with a generalized critical review which the critic must force his "weary brain and hands to write." But the critic must "seek a meaning to the mystery, that veils I know not what believable." In this search he goes beyond Ulysses, challenging him: "Thou refused/The music manifest, and I refuse/Thy misty surmise of the Unutterable." For the sake of his search, the critic will risk the song of the sirens. He seeks not so much truth as the vision, and he rejects the philosopher Plato for the poet Plato. He will suffer in experience his personal destiny: "I will be/The master of my soul's lost harmony."[20]

Perhaps his best imaginative work is his second play, *Cinnamon and Angelica* (1920), written at the end of the experience of World War I and republished with slight changes in 1941. It is appropriate to modern war in its theme—a stray shot kills the man whose love brought peace—and in the emphasis on the minuteness of man in a vast destructive world. In *Between Two Worlds* Murry speaks of the source of the play in a simultaneous feeling of the infinite littleness of things human with the utmost pang of human desire and disappointment (it was for this reason that characters were given the names of spices). Murry is struck with wonder that out of the small game of human life—insignificant, subject to quick disappearance—can come such greatness of love and beauty: "I do scarce believe/ There's any issue in this life of ours/Save its own poignant beauty."[21]

In general, one might say that in Murry's creative work there is perplexity without solution. He was not enough of an artist to supply an esthetic resolution to a thoughtful and troubled mind. He was better when he studied and interpreted the profundity of artists who had achieved a form of resolution. The first book in which he displayed his real talent was *Fyodor Dostoevsky: A Critical Study* (1916).

III *The Russian Soul*

Murry describes the manner of his writing *Fyodor Dostoevsky: A Critical Study* in his autobiography. The book had been commissioned two years earlier in order to pay off a debt to a publisher, but it had been delayed because Murry found that he "had nothing really to say about Dostoevsky." He even solicited Lawrence's help in suggesting ideas about the Russian author, but fortunately Lawrence's notes about ideas were delayed; for, in his own thinking about Dostoevsky, Murry suddenly found his true critical orientation:

I had read all Dostoevsky's major books over three times, first with a glimmering of comprehension and finally with an altogether unprecedented flood of illumination. Suddenly the whole thing had fallen into pattern; and I was, for the first time, the victim of the strange sensation of being hardly more than the amanuensis of a book that wrote itself. To a person of my peculiar composition such an experience was an inward revolution. For the first time in my life, I had the experience of certitude. It was no question of my opinion of Dostoevsky; I had no opinion of Dostoevsky: and if I expressed any personal opinions about him in the book, they were certainly exaggerated and probably wrong. All that had happened—I speak, of course, of my sensation only—was that the objective "pattern" of Dostoevsky had declared itself, through me as instrument.[22]

The book reveals, perhaps, the haste of a revelatory style, but it has a unity of theme and an originality of approach which makes it an interesting and readable contribution. It sets the pattern for Murry's more important work on Keats and Shakespeare and for his approach to general works such as *Heaven—and Earth*. Looking back at it some fifteen years later, Murry could say it was "immature, extravagant, and excessively 'intellectual,' " but that "in the essential" he stood by it.[23]

Murry emphasizes that he is not concerned with literary criticism in a formal sense. He is concerned "only to think of what may be for us prophetic in it."[24] Like Anatole France, he sees in great literature the adventure of a soul; but Murry wants purpose in the adventure, so that the works of the author become evolutionary in that each one is a stage in the total pattern of the author's mind and thought. The virtue of this method is an enthusiasm for literature as most deeply involved with human life; one can feel Murry's earnestness and his exhilarating sense of dealing with greatness. The danger is that the evolutionary approach may demand concessions to its own logic, or it may appear to have too close a relationship to the evolution of the critic's own life. This charge can be made against Murry in some of his writings, but he frequently saves himself from such charges by his constant and sensitive reference to the works he is discussing. He was seeking an answer to the question—as he felt Dostoevsky was— "What must I do to be saved?" but he was seeing the question in terms of the regeneration of mankind rather than in terms of personal salvation. The plan of his study is to follow the evolution of Dosteovsky's great novels, each one of which "seems to mark an epoch in the human consciousness," until the final vision in *The Brothers Karamazov*.

His system works well as he follows the male protagonists through Dostoevsky's most important works. First, Murry understands Dostoevsky in *Crime and Punishment* as imagining what will happen when he frees the human will from conventional morality and an accepted God. Roskolnikov tries to assert a pure personal will by reassuring himself that he can commit the perfect murder, justify it rationally (he frees society from a "louse," an evil old pawnbroker who preys on her fellowmen), and remain untroubled by guilt or fear of punishment. But he cannot do it: he can reason his way to freedom, but he has not the will to achieve it. He never spiritually gets outside the "City of Good." He is subject to this city's values and he is finally punished by it.

The more important figure in this book, Murry maintains, is Svidrigailov, who is able to do what Raskolnikov could not: he goes beyond good and evil. He appears to us as a monster because of his depravity, but he can do "good" as easily as he can do "evil" because "he is his own right" acting from his own pure "single will."[25] Svidrigailov, says Murry, was Dostoevsky's "new word" in literature, "the beginning of his own peculiar development"[26]—"the symbol of Dostoevsky's passionate denial of God, when he had looked on pain."[27] Dostoevsky poses the question of whether there can be a Will beyond the human will in this world of pain (which would suggest that any Will beyond is evil), and he uses Svidrigailov for this test:

Svidrigailov has dared to face life alone, to measure his individual will against all things. And at the last he is broken. He is conscious of his utter loneliness. He has dared to try the great issue. He has done what he knows to be evil, so that he might know whether there was some power beyond him that should punish. He does know: he has not been blasted. Yes, he would have had a flush of ecstatic happiness thrill his soul, if when he did evil he had been struck dead. But no, nothing. . . .[28]

So in a scene almost comic in its dry matter-of-factness, Svidrigailov shoots himself.

One attempt to discover the right path of conduct, via the assertion of the individual will, had led to despair. Dostoevsky, says Murry, tries the other path—not the assertion, but the annihilation of individual will, the willingness to suffer. Dostoevsky tries this in the creation of Myshkin in *The Idiot*. Myshkin is the Christ-like, all-suffering figure in whom passion becomes compassion, in whom willful passion becomes the Christian passion, an endless suffering of the burdens of others. To the world, he is the idiot who does not fight or answer back and who consorts with prostitutes and murderers, accepting the punishment which they and disapproving society heap upon him. Murry sees in Myshkin the end, for Dostoevsky, of the epoch of tragedy; the end of the unconquerable hope on which tragedy is based. There is no purification, only annihilation, an annihilation of will which, in the end, is only complementary to the assertion of the will, culminating in an equally vain despair: "The will which wills its own annihilation in a life of suffering comes to no other end than the will which wills its supreme assertion. The human perfection of Myshkin and the inhuman perfection of Svidrigailov are turned alike to derision. To do evil and to suffer it—each is vanity."[29]

How to transcend this impasse? Before coming to his final vision in *The Brothers Karamazov*, Dostoevsky had to go to the limits of human consciousness. This, says Murry, Dostoevsky does in the figure of Stavrogin in *The Possessed*: "In Stavrogin he had gone his lonely way to the ultimate outpost of the present Dispensation."[30] Stavrogin is the ultimate in the expression of modern man in will and knowledge. In him, Dostoevsky returns to the willful type of Svidrigailov but gives him a supreme awareness in addition to action: ". . . to sacrifice all things to his will, all instincts, all impulses, all emotions, all loves, all loyalties; . . . to be in all things conscious, since to yield to that which was unconscious was to declare himself a slave to the life which he hated and denied; to will that his own will should be the master absolute of all things. . . ."[31]

Stavrogin continues in this willfulness until he, like Svidrigailov, defeats himself. For his will demands that his pride should yield; and, when he breaks his pride, "he had killed even that which had urged him to kill his pride. The spring of the will itself was broken. There was not only nothing left to will, but of the will itself nothing remained."[32] The human will, in fact, can will to annihilate itself; and human knowledge (covering science and reason) can assist in this annihilation since it can pervert a person's attempt to dedicate himself to a dream or ideal which contains an element of falsity: "Stavrogin was weak because he was so strong that he could not deceive himself."[33] With Stavrogin's suicide, claims Murry, "the last hope of consciousness and conscious will is gone."[34] All that Dostoevsky can hope for is "the miracle" of the new dispensation.

In *The Brothers Karamazov,* Dostoevsky comes to his final vision in the attempt to define the new dispensation. Murry sees the main characters basically as representations of past, present, and future; old Fyodor Karamazov, the father, is a pure sensualist, "the blind force of life" or "chaos unresolved."[35] He lives under the old Dispensation; it is for his sons to become articulate and aware, which they do in different ways. They all inherit the sensual nature of the father, but they must suffer consciousness of what they are doing. Dimitri, like his father, follows the dictates of his physical nature—he has violent physical reactions of love and hate; but he has also "a vision of some harmony and beauty which he may attain through the body."[36] (The meaning of "body" in relation to "soul" and "spirit" was a continual concern for Murry—and was, in fact, at the root of his disagreement with Lawrence.) Dimitri's generous nature, based on instinct and intuition, is insufficient for him to achieve his goal, so he turns to Ivan, "the mind," for guidance. Where "Dimitri is body conscious of mind, Ivan is mind conscious of body."[37] The two brothers represent the present Dispensation, Ivan being especially relevant as the complicated modern intellectual: "in him the seeking mind is borne onwards to what seems like a delirium of abstract speculation,"[38] the climax in the novel being the dialogue with the Grand Inquisitor. Ivan is torn between affirmation and rebellion, capable of performing an act of heroic virtue without believing in virtue. "So in both Ivan and Dimitri is manifest the failure of the divided being of the present Dispensation." The reconciliation, the man of the new Dispensation, comes with the third brother,

Alyosha. He brings into harmony all that is understood by body and mind: "he has the waking consciousness of the harmony of all things."[39] Alyosha is the man to be, "the promise of all humanity."[40] Dostoevsky accepts that Alyosha can only be understood, in view of the pain and suffering and disillusionment and suicidal despair of his earlier heroes, as "a miracle in time." For Murry, however, the miraculous is not the denial but the fulfillment of human consciousness.

Such is the main theme of Murry's book. Murry follows his theme into more subtle byways, such as the differences in the same type—comparisons, for example, of Stavrogin and Ivan Karamazov, and of Myshkin and Alyosha—but the main pattern, the evolving career of Dostoevsky as "God-seeker," is basic to Murry's own way of life. There is in Murry, perhaps, too much "God-seeking" or too much cerebral determination of a "God-seeking" pattern—it is "on his mind" too much. Katherine Mansfield's humorous remark is apposite here: "Jack can't fry a sausage without thinking about God!"[41]

Apparently both she and Lawrence objected to the Dostoevsky who appealed to Murry, "the arch-hierophant of intellectual self-consciousness."[42] In his journal Murry describes an evening with Mansfield and Lawrence:

It started with Dostoevsky. Lawrence was all against him for his humility and love. It was the search for the Absolute everywhere, as though all individuals might at the last be reduced to a common ether. I retorted that the love was but a means of ascertaining the individual quality of the individual ether, in the sense that it made communication possible. Katherine was quite violent in condemnation of Dostoevsky's "open house for foolish people." Lawrence was even more explosive. "Humility is Death. To believe in an Absolute is Death. There are no Absolutes." Katherine was eager in agreement with this. I wanted to ask her what she meant but wisely refrained.[43]

When Murry sent the book to him, Lawrence repeated his objections: "You've got the cart before the horse," he told Murry. "It isn't the being that must follow the mind, but the mind must follow the being." He continued in a caustic way about people who dig their heads in the sand like the disgusting ostrich to see a revelation there.[44] Murry was young and wrote his book in the heyday of the fashionable cult of the "Russian soul"; Professor Dorothy Brewster in her *East-West Passage* observes that, "while the fever lasted, Mr. Murry ran perhaps the highest temperature."[45]

It is true that there was a fever about the "Russian soul" which in many ways we now see to have been critically naïve, but it did undoubtedly have a good effect in rejuvenating English ideas about literature. It is noteworthy that the first book of importance which Murry published was on Russian literature, at a time when, because of his editing especially, he was in the midst of English literary circles, and when he had recently been in the midst of French literary circles in Paris, reviewing French books. Yet he felt, apparently, that much of the spirit had gone out of English Romanticism and French Classicism— or that worse, the English were making an esthetic philosophy of a lifeless "Flaubertian" technical method.[46] Shortly after World War I Murry was writing such essays as "The Defeat of Imagination,"[47] and making such statements on the civilization in which he found himself as "it is not a civilisation at all. It is a material condition which has usurped a spiritual title."[48] Into this atmosphere the works of Tolstoy, Dostoevsky, and Chekhov came like gifts from the gods, revealing new sources of hope and energy; and Murry "went overboard" in appreciation and gratitude.

The two essays, "The Honesty of Russia"[49] and "The Dream of a Queer Fellow,"[50] written in 1916, reveal the new sense of purpose which reading the Russians gave to Murry. At this period, Murry's question "Is life worth living?"[51] must have been asked countless times; and Murry finds the reply in the sense of life of the Russian writers: "the great assumption which they made, at least in the beginning of the quest, was that to live life must mean to live it wholly.... To them life was the sum of all human potentialities."[52] In the same way art must have seemed of small concern in the middle of World War I, yet the Russian writers believed that "somehow art is the supreme human activity."[53] For Murry, the Russians had rediscovered the vital connection between art and the spiritual life, then and always one of his main concerns: "the Russian soul is tormented by problems to which we have long been dead, and to which we need to be alive again."[54]

CHAPTER 2

Murry, Eliot, and Style

IN 1922 Murry gave a lecture in which he said that "there are moments when criticism of a particular kind, the only kind I care for, utterly absorbs me. I feel that I am touching a mystery. There is a wall, as it were, of dense, warm darkness before me—a darkness which is secretly alive and thrilling to the sense. This, I believe, is the reflection in myself of the darkness which broods over the poet's creative mind. It forms slowly and gradually gathers while I read his work. The sense of mystery deepens and deepens; but the quality of the mystery be-- comes more plain. There is a moment when, as though unconsciously and out of my control, the deeper rhythm of a poet's work, the rise and fall of the great moods which determined what he was and what he wrote, enter into me also. I feel his presence; I am obedient to it, and it seems to me as though the breathing of my spirit is at one with his."[1]

The tone of this passage—the sense of "mystery," the identification with another presence—makes it sound more like an account of a mystical process than a critical apologia. Yet, during the same period, Murry wrote an essay in which he asserted: "The secret lies in Aristotle. The true literary critic must have a humanistic philosophy.... This is why we have to go back to the Greeks for the principles of art and criticism, and why only those critics who have returned to bathe themselves in the life-giving source have made enduring contributions to criticism."[2]

On the basis of this statement, Murry could be judged a twentieth-century Neo-Classic, and there are passages in his practical criticism which would support this judgment. Yet both quotations are typical. With Murry, one has to accept the reality of the two sides of his attitude: Aristotle's intellectual analysis has somehow to live with the medieval Meister Eckhart's faithful acceptance of mystery. Murry is the author of books on

the Romantic visionary Blake as well as the Classicist church-
man Swift, and he expressed the mystical element in his criticism in a collection of essays called *Discoveries,* the title used by
the arch-Classicist Ben Jonson.

Murry himself, it should be noted, did not feel the separation
of the mystic in him from the artist or critic. For Murry,
Baudelaire's remark, "La première condition nécessaire pour
faire un art sain est la croyance à l'unité intégrale"—"the primary condition essential to create a healthy art is belief in in-
tegral unity"—is basically of the same order as the sense of one-
ness, the "at-one-ment" of the religious mystic; and Meister
Eckhart's saintly vision of "God in all things" is akin to Keats's
observation, "I have loved the principle of beauty in all things."[3]
But Murry's insistence on essential unity—whether in the realm
of criticism or not—did not prevent him from applying his
Classical training and making intellectual distinctions useful to
criticism. As it was, he was too easily dismissed because of the
element of mysticism in his nature. Early in his career, in 1927,
he notes that his reputation as an "intellectual" has been replaced: "Now, if I have any reputation, it is simply that of a
mystic, as I am called by those who are kind to me, or of an
emotional crank, as I am called by those who are not. My own
opinion is that I have become a reasonable man."[4]

Although he was not dismissed by the more important
writers of the time, such as T. S. Eliot and D. H. Lawrence,
they were wary of Murry's mysticism. While paying tribute to
Murry's critical ability, Eliot made fun of his "inner voice" approach;[5] and Lawrence, who also was quick to recognize
Murry's talents, objected strongly when Murry made him appear
as a writer with a mysterious "sixth sense."[6] Certainly, in relation to Murry's later development, it would be difficult to disagree with the general verdict that, after the 1920's, there was a
decline in him as a literary critic as he became increasingly involved in religion and social affairs. Sir Richard Rees, who
knew Murry well, claims that this development was inevitable:
"It is sometimes said that he would have done better to confine
himself to literary subjects. But he was a mystic, and his mysticism was of a kind which made a life-long specialisation in
literary criticism impossible."[7]

At the same time, there was a positive value for Murry, even for criticism, in this psychological dichotomy; the tension between his mystical sensitivity and Classical intelligence which proved his weakness in later years also proved his strength in the prevailing negativism and loss of direction in the years following World War I. Several critics, looking back over that period, have commented on the value of Murry's work. Sir Herbert Read has called him "the most stimulating 'creative' critic" of the time,[8] and another reviewer has applauded "his insight into literature as a composite appeal to the reader's entire nature, which helped to reawaken confidence in poetry and fiction, as a medium for the intelligence of the age at a time of dejection and uncertainty."[9]

The lectures, essays and reviews published in *The Times Literary Supplement, The Athenæum, The Adelphi* and other periodicals and collected in such volumes as *Aspects of Literature* (1920), *The Problem of Style* (1922), the two volumes of *Countries of the Mind* (1922 and 1931), *Discoveries* (1924), and *To the Unknown God* (1924) are a remarkable achievement, somewhat similar in function to Sir Philip Sidney's *Defence of Poesie,* to Wordsworth's Preface to *The Lyrical Ballads,* and to Matthew Arnold's *Essays:* they help to articulate the consciousness of the age and to suggest paths for future literary and cultural development. The epithet "creative" which Read applies to Murry is much abused nowadays, but it is useful in distinguishing his criticism from that which is found more commonly in academic circles. Murry's criticism was of the kind which led to a creative atmosphere for writers and to wide literary appreciation rather than to the academy.* His tastes in later life demonstrate this difference: on the one hand, he had little sympathy with the scholarly critics loosely termed

---

* J. H. Watson, in a tribute in *The London Magazine* (May, 1959) entitled, "A Good Workman and his Friends: Recollections of John Middleton Murry," tells from his own experience how the world of Keats and Shakespeare, Chekhov and Hardy, Lawrence and Murry was opened up for a group of pit workers by *The Adelphi* magazine. "All kinds of people were attracted to his work," Watson writes. "A railway signalman once stopped me in the street and said, 'I believe you know Middleton Murry. He is my arch-priest.'"

"the new critics," and, on the other, he was excited to discover the work of J. D. Salinger. In fact, the combination of a moral concern with society and a personal, frequently mystical, enquiry into religious values, which one finds in Salinger and other modern American writers, was just that which was basic to Murry's own work.

One point is certain. However one judges the critical attitude of Murry, there is no doubt that it enabled him to be an outstanding editor and "talent-scout." He was sensitive to the quality of genius and was articulate enough to guide an audience to some understanding of genius. He helped to reveal the greatness in Paul Valéry, Marcel Proust, James Joyce, Thomas Hardy as poet, Wilfred Owen, George Santayana, Gerard Manley Hopkins, and Eliot. Some of these writers were introduced by Murry to a British public, and that public was a much wider one than is usually reached by serious literary magazines.

I *The Eliot-Murry Debate*

An approach to an understanding of Murry's point of view and of his place in literary history can be made through one of the most interesting encounters of modern times, the strangely neglected debate between T. S. Eliot and Middleton Murry, which lasted nearly forty years. From one aspect, this debate is probably the best version of the old Romanticism-Classicism clash brought into the twentieth century; from another, the two men complement rather than oppose each other, the issues of modern criticism seeming to indicate that they disagreed only within the framework of a similar commitment.

As previously noted, Murry invited Eliot in 1919 to be an assistant editor on *The Athenæum*, solely on the basis of the impression that Eliot's first book, *Prufrock and Other Observations*, had made on him. Eliot declined, and later became editor of *The Criterion*, while Murry became editor of *The Adelphi*. The argument that is central to their difference occurred in 1923 in an exchange between these two magazines. Murry wrote a somewhat hasty and light essay in his *Adelphi* which asserted that "there is no point, in English conditions, in opposing Romanticism to Classicism. In England there never has been any classicism worth talking about: we have had our classics, but no classicism. And all our classics are romantic."[10] The reason for this romanticism is that "individualism ... is in our British bones":

The English writer, the English divine, the English statesman, inherit no rules from their forbears: they inherit only this: a sense that in the last resort they must depend upon the inner voice. If they dig deep enough in their pursuit of self-knowledge—a piece of mining done not with the intellect alone, but with the whole man—they will come upon a self that is universal: in religious terms, the English tradition is that the man who truly interrogates himself will ultimately hear the voice of God, in terms of literary criticism, the writer achieves impersonality through personality.[11]

It was not difficult for Eliot to criticize—even to make fun of— this statement, especially of the first part. The "inner voice," he retorted in *The Criterion,* "sounds remarkably like an old principle which has been formulated by an elder critic in the now familiar phrase of 'doing as one likes.' The possessors of the inner voice ride ten in a compartment to a football match at Swansea, listening to the inner voice, which breathes the eternal message of vanity, fear, and lust."[12]

If the argument is left at this stage—and it too frequently is—the advantage would seem to be with Eliot. Murry, it might be said, is the perfect candidate to illustrate T. E. Hulme's definition of Romanticism as "spilt religion." But, as one frequently finds with Murry, statements which appear on the surface to be simple, and even ill-considered, are in fact the result of continued meditation. Murry replied to Eliot in a more serious essay, "More about Romanticism."[13]

In this essay, Murry accepts that, on an ideal level, Romanticism and Classicism—in the terms of the definitions in the argument, namely that the "essential attitude" of Romanticism is "an obedience to the inner voice" and of Classicism "obedience to an external spiritual authority"—are mutually exclusive. But, first, he insists that the question must be considered in its historical setting. Can we *choose* today to be Classic or Romantic? Murry maintains that we cannot. The element of choice is not on this plane. Today we are in an epoch, says Murry, which began with the Renaissance and Reformation, in which the individual "vindicated his right to stand or fall by his own experience, to explore the universe for himself."[14] This personal exploration by "the experiencing self" (the phrase is taken from Walter Bagehot) is, he argues, the beginning of Romanticism and the English literary tradition. We are in a world of Romantic consciousness, and it is within this consciousness that we must confront such issues as the clash of the "external universe" with the "internal universe." We have to explore both universes and bear the paradox which such exploration burdens us with. We cannot escape by thinking we can choose; in other words, the arguments for or against adopting a Romantic or Classic attitude are, for practical purposes, irrelevant.

Next, Murry deals more specifically with the significance of the "inner voice." Is Eliot right in asserting that it means "doing as one likes"? Even if Eliot's interpretation is allowed, is the irony misplaced—is it, in fact, easy or undesirable to "do as one likes"? Murry begins by redefining what we as "experiencing selves" mean by the "external" world and the "internal." By "external," he says, we must mean that realm in which our choice is not free, because of authority or necessity; and by "internal," that realm in which the self is free: "The paradox is this: as man seeks to know the universe, he finds outside him a realm of necessity and within him a realm of freedom; and he finds, moreover, that to know the external world as a world of necessity is the necessary condition of knowing it at all, and likewise that to know the internal world as a world of freedom is the necessary condition for knowing it at all."[15]

Murry agrees that it is a grave error to ignore necessity and to escape into a world of illusion or try to explain one world in terms of the other; and herein, Murry maintains, lay Rousseau's mistake. Rousseau should not have said, "man is born free: he is everywhere in chains," but "man *is* free; and he is everywhere subject to necessity."[16] We cannot avoid being confronted by this paradox; the question is how, if at all, are we going to resolve it?

In the first place, Murry agrees with Eliot to the extent that he deplores a weak kind of Romanticism, in which the "primary Romantic," as he terms him, has an immediate experience, perhaps a genuine enough mystical perception; but he attempts to resolve the paradox by retiring defiantly into "the fortress of the ego" and proclaiming that the world of necessity is subject to his own kingdom of freedom. Murry's condemnation of the thoughtless and egocentric in criticism should be emphasized; on another occasion he deplored "the impressionistic criticism which has sapped the English brain for a generation past."[17]

However, there is the mature "secondary Romantic," Murry continues, who knows that an intuitive insight is not a comprehensive truth, but only a hint of the possibility of a greater human consciousness. He knows that we cannot at present apprehend the world of experience save under "contradictory categories,"[18] but he accepts the promise, which his moments of vision give him, of a resolution of the basic human paradox under the new dispensation, "the brave new world," which, for example, is pointed to by Shakespeare, Tolstoy, and Dostoevsky.

Mature Romanticism, Murry insists, is not, whatever the Neo-Classicists say, libertarian or egalitarian, or a surrender to the vain ego; for "not only does it demand the surrender of myself to my self, but it demands that I should surrender to achieved completeness in others."[19] This generous surrender of self is the means to fulfillment and also the means by which the personal broadens to the impersonal. Or, to make the point another way, Murry allows Eliot's argument that Romanticism allows one "to do what you like." But, he argues, there is nothing to scoff at in this; "to do what you like" is very difficult:

For to know what you really like means to know what you really are; and that is a matter of painful experience and slow exploration. To discover that within myself that I *must* obey, to gain some awareness of the law which operates in the organic whole of the internal world, to feel this internal world as an organic whole working out its own destiny according to some secret vital principle, to know which acts and utterances are a liberation from obstacles and an accession of strength, to acknowledge secret loyalties which one cannot deny without impoverishment and starvation—this is to possess one's soul indeed, and it is not easy either to do or explain. And yet, I believe that it can be done without deceiving oneself; and I also believe that we have the faculty of recognising instantly when another has achieved this consummation.[20]

It is in this communion of insight that Murry sees the special contribution of Romanticism, and that he finds his primary function as critic. His task was to discover and then work from the "creative centre" of the writer. The greater the writer, the more mystical is the apprehension of the "creative centre," since the greatest artistic perceptions are those moments of "immediate apprehension of the unity of the world" in which the basic paradox is resolved; freedom and necessity are united in a single organic whole: "the 'mystical' vision is a vision of *organic* necessity" and it is "at the creative centre of Wordsworth of Shelley, of Keats, and of Coleridge."[21] This conception, it might be noted, has a Classical echo, in that the living organism for Murry is defined as that which *necessarily* wills to follow "its own inward law of life,"[22] reminding one of those high moments of tragedy in which the protagonist *chooses* what he *has* to do, and there is the coming together of free will and fate.

It is not perhaps the "logic" of a mystical approach which is of concern so much as the quality and attitude of mind which the "arguments" reveal, and the extent to which the theory proves itself successfully in practice. For example, T. S. Eliot, in what is no doubt meant to be a favorable foreword to the posthumously published collection of Murry's essays, is scarcely adequate when he describes Murry's kind of criticism as that which, "in exploring the mind and soul of some creative writer, explored his own mind and soul also."[23] This statement could mean little more than that Murry used writers, especially great ones, as stepping-stones in a kind of vicarious self-expression. It does not give a sense of the real, even selfless, dedication which Murry gave to the writers he criticized.

In this attitude, in fact, there was a basic difference from Eliot, whose own criticism, as he admitted, "is a by-product of his creative activity."[24] And Eliot's remark that his criticism should be viewed in relation to his poetry is illustrated by his various and changing attitudes to Milton. Murry also disapproved of Milton in some ways; however, there was no question of relating this attitude to his own work, but, by comparison, to the authors to whom he had dedicated himself—to Shakespeare, Keats, and Blake in particular. His criticism was not a "by-product": his creative act was to introduce us to the greatness and spirit of the originals.

Eliot is undoubtedly right in stating that Middleton Murry "was a literary critic first and foremost,"[25] and this point needs to be emphasized. Murry sees the center of life in the work of the great writers he admired. He does not come from outside, as it were, as one who is primarily a religious mystic and who is searching for quotations to support his viewpoint. He resented, in fact, any attempt to classify him as a religious man *using* poetry. In his well-known *Prière et Poèsie,* Henri Brémond gives pride of place to Murry as a critic who uses poetry to find a path of salvation. But in his review of Brémond's book, Murry balks at the emphasis on mystical religion, and comments, somewhat curtly, that "there is plenty of mystery in poetry without making it mystical."[26]

For Murry, "the poem is our datum;"[27] he is concerned with the form and style of art in its own right, though never, of course, apart from the rest of life. In a passage echoing Aristotle's famous statement on the relationship of poetry to other disciplines, Murry observes: "between belief and logic lies a third kingdom, which the mystics and philosophers alike are too eager to forget—the kingdom of art, no less the residence of truth than the two other realms, and to some, perhaps, more authentic even than they."[28]

Unless one accepts this primacy of the fact of the literary work with Murry, one finds it difficult to explain the undoubted —and continuing—success of his collection of lectures on the subject of style.[29] He is concerned with style, and in a way which corresponds with Eliot's basic approach; he takes the view that the words of literary art are a means of conveying a message of some importance from the individual artist to an audience: the task of the poets is "so to mate the world to an entire mental experience that its similar is aroused in their readers"[30]— a statement which could be a definition of Eliot's "objective correlative."

We must return to Murry's work on style, but, for the sake of completeness, it might be useful first to review other aspects of his relationship with Eliot. As already noted, Murry's great contribution in the 1920's was, in large part, to restore confidence in the purpose of literature, and even in the purpose of the future; it is not therefore surprising that, although he greatly admired Eliot's talent, he was appalled by the tone of barren despair of much of Eliot's poetry. In an article with the ironic title "The 'Classical Revival' "[31] he classes Eliot with the "Bloomsbury Group" and their "absolute skepticism." He considers both *The Waste Land* and Virginia Woolf's *Jacob's Room* as failures in that the effect of both was "the exercise of a prodigious intellectual subtlety to produce the effect of a final futility." He sees no future in such works. In *The Waste Land* he finds a clash between principles and content—there is no order in the nihilism; and "The Hollow Men" is even more barren.

As Murry in ensuing years became increasingly interested in religious and social concerns, he found himself more and more at odds with the views of Eliot. He disliked this widening schism between intellectuals and intellectual ideas as being somehow unnatural; he could not accept Eliot's principle of "separation." It might be mentally possible to separate philosophy, religion, and poetry; but in the living process of existence it was impossible. There was a more important principle of unity. At one time Murry made an effort to overcome "the wasteful distribution of intellectual forces" by suggesting that, although the old Thomistic synthesis could not be revivified in the modern world, a new synthesis was possible in which "intelligence" and "intuition" would be subsumed under a fresh concept of "reason." One effect of this would be to transcend the Classicism-Romanticism debate. His essay "Towards a Synthesis" attracted considerable attention when it appeared in *The Criterion* in 1927, but it proved quite unconvincing to Eliot and others.[32]

Yet, in perspective, there appears as much complementarity as division in the different views of Eliot and Murry—the high Anglican conservative is complemented by Murry, whom Eliot once described as "a rare survival of that almost extinct species, the genuine heretic."[33] In spite of growing divergences of opinion, Murry always sensed a kinship. In 1920 he had told Katherine Mansfield that Eliot was the only critic of literature he thought anything of;[34] and in 1931, he wrote, "With very few of my contemporaries have I felt myself, at one crucial moment and another, more deeply in sympathy than with Mr. Eliot: so that it has often seemed to me that we had the same realisations, but that, by some trick of destiny or idiosyncrasy, the effect of those realisations upon us was antipodal."[35] Then in 1954 Murry wrote in his journal that he and Eliot "lived in the same *kind* of isolation. Not that I could really enter his world, or he mine; but there was a strange feeling of kinship between us."[36]

It is perhaps easier to explain this feeling of kinship from the distance of the modern critical scene than it was for Murry. The battles over such concepts as Romanticism and Classicism, which occupied much of their energy, seem largely of the past. There is as much, or more, significance in their points of agreement. Mr. Lea, in his biography of Murry, has found a very good instance of this, which is worth quoting in full, especially in view of Murry's published criticism of *The Waste Land:*

The essay on "Russian Literature" concludes with a passage on Tchehov:
" 'Good-bye, my treasure!' There is the magic that makes a paradise of a desert of human hopes. We look again, we listen: yes, the harmony is there. And if the harmony is where Tchehov found it, then it is everywhere. He is, in the great company of men of genius, the latest-born. He comes, the youngest son, and there is no inheritance for him. The great estate of human life has been divided: so he goes off alone into the waste and desolate places, the dreary commonplace wildernesses of the spirit, which are as like the wildernesses of the heroic writers, as the waste ground in a modern city is like the majestic jungles of the Amazon. Tchehov goes there, without hope, without belief; it is the last of all forlorn quests: and he brings back the Grail in his hands."
It was after he had just written these words, Murry always remembered, that, glancing at the *Literary Supplement,* he caught sight of the announcement of a new poem by Eliot, entitled *The Waste Land.* The coincidence so struck him that he wrote to Eliot, who came down to Selsfield, and, to his further surprise, informed him that there was a traditional, even technical, connection between the Waste Land and the Grail—on which, indeed, his poem was based. "I came nearer to Tom Eliot in that day than I had ever been before, or ever was afterwards."[37]

"The Waste Land and the Grail"—the phrase provides a fair representation of the cultural climate in which Murry and Eliot found themselves. They were living in a disillusioned world, and both were concerned with a search for the means to spiritual reconstruction. Their ways were different, but they were both "Christ-centred" in their attitudes to life and literature; and they were aware of a sense of commitment. Basically, in fact, both approaches were ethical in that they chose and knew their choice; in this commitment lies their main distinction from much of modern criticism. Northrop Frye has expressed this new grouping—in which Murry and Eliot appear on the same side in opposition to a more scientific or "uncommitted" school of critics—in a comment on Eliot's essay, "The Function of Criticism." In this essay Eliot refers to "Middleton Murry, who is spoken of approvingly because 'he is aware that there are definite positions to be taken, and that now and then one must actually reject something and select something else.' There are [Frye retorts] no definite positions to be taken in chemistry or philology, and if there are any to be taken in criticism, criticism is not a field of genuine learning."[38] Perhaps all that one can say at this point is that Murry was just not Frye's kind of critic. Murry might have begun to answer Frye by agreeing more or less with the last statement—that criticism is not *primarily* a field of learning. Murry deplored the loss of the amateur quality in criticism for this reason. He liked to quote Chekhov's comment that the greatest writers have always had axes to grind.[39] One of the functions of the disciple-critic was to help the master convey his message.

II *The Problem of Style*

Murry showed his basic Classicism in his advice that the critic should return to Aristotle.[40] At the same time, it was Plato rather than Aristotle who temperamentally appealed to him, and he makes his Aristotle sound idealistically "Platonic": "The living centre of Aristotle's criticism is a conception of art as a means to a good life.... Indeed, it would not be an exaggeration to say that the very pith and marrow of Aristotle's literary criticism is a system of moral values derived from his contemplation of life.... The imitation of life in literature was for Aristotle, the creative revelation of the ideal actively at work in human life."[41]

In the same essay, Murry dismissed the French "sterilised and lifeless Aristotelianism which has been the plague of criticism for centuries."[42] There was, of course, a more positive side to French Neo-Classic formalism than Murry indicates, but one has frequently to allow for the easy journalistic generalizations in Murry, especially when, as here, he is answering T. S. Eliot, who had put forward Aristotle, Dryden, and Coleridge as model literary critics. Murry eliminates Dryden because he was too greatly influenced by the "dead mechanical framework of rules" which characterized French criticism—as contrasted with Coleridge's organic approach.

Whatever his approach to Aristotle, Murry's basic pattern of thinking was classically Aristotelian insofar as he regarded literature as existing in its own right with its own laws and, at the same time, as owing its existence to its middle place between two other realms. In a paraphrase of Aristotle's famous remark on the relation of poetry to history and philosophy, one might say that, for Murry, literature was more logical than mystery and more mysterious than logic. Literature, also, has a very concrete existence; it is, says Murry, a "crystallization";[43] and the nature of this crystallization is the style of the writer.

Again like Aristotle, Murry emphasizes the primary importance of metaphor in literary style. In his several passages on metaphor, which are among his best work, he rescues metaphor from being considered a rhetorical device and makes it a poetical necessity. He does not deny—in fact, he emphasizes—the artificiality of literature; but he distinguishes this literary artifice from rhetorical structure, the difference being in sincerity. This problem of sincerity is, indeed, his first consideration in the six lectures collected as *The Problem of Style*,[44] a justly popular book. In theme and tone, this work is reminiscent of the Classic treatise *On the Sublime* by "Longinus," being an examination of how greatness has been achieved in literature, with general comments liberally illustrated by an analysis of examples from great literature. There is a sense of Longinus too, in the author's unquestionable love of literature, with its power to "transport" the reader.

In trying to give a basic definition of style, Murry meets the usual difficulty. He is at pains to distinguish it from the ornamental; and, while allowing that "style" may be used for personal idiosyncrasy or technique, he thinks of it ideally: "absolute style is the complete realisation of a universal significance in a personal and particular expression."[45] Like Dr. Johnson, Murry is concerned with literature as a means to basic truths, but he begins with the personal and emotive. He quotes approvingly Remy de Gourmont: "The whole effort of a sincere man is to erect his personal impressions into universal laws."[46] Sincerity and sensitivity in personal contact with life is, it sometimes seems, all that the writer needs; it is dangerous to try the tricks of rhetoric—the true writer finds his style as part of the organic process of creation: "The lesson of the masters is really unanimous. Feel, see, they say with one voice, and the rest shall be added unto you."[47]

Murry was acutely aware of the dangers—especially during the period in which he lived—of a loose impression vaguely expressed. Just as he insisted on complete and open sincerity in experience, so he insisted on the greatest possible precision in expression. As to how this preciseness should be achieved, he refers to a favorite quotation from Stendhal: "Style is this: to add to a given thought all the circumstances fitted to produce the whole effect that the thought ought to produce."[48] Murry recognizes that, for his purposes, the modern word "thought" is insufficient here—Stendhal's use of it had a wider application. Murry defines it as a general term to cover "intuitions, convictions, perceptions, and their accompanying emotions";[49] and the "circumstances" which Stendhal says must be added are for Murry "the emotional field."

Murry himself uses words more precisely than he has been given credit for. It is misleading to dismiss his theories easily as being based on "emotion." First, he is in a long tradition in the use of the word, as an examination of the use of *movere* and derivitives in Renaissance criticism can demonstrate; and, second, he expands "emotion" to serve not just as the basis of a lyric but also of longer dramatic and narrative work. "Emotion" is not merely an immediate feeling but a "mode of experience" based upon a subtle interplay and development of original emotions. Moreover, with this increasingly complex development, there grows a progressively acute understanding of the human situation in general: "It is by virtue of this mysterious accumulation of past emotions that the writer, in his maturity, is able to accomplish the miracle of giving to the particular the weight and force of the universal."[50]

Such a view bears obvious affinities with Wordsworth's view as expressed in the Preface to the Second Edition of *The Lyrical Ballads,* and Murry acknowledges this kinship; and part of the value of his exploration is that he encourages us to reconsider the Romantic theorists. At the same time, he is reiterating his critical process: if every writer has a basic quality in his attitude to life, or "mode of experience," then the critic's first job is to know the writer he is criticizing "until he is saturated with his mode of experience."[51] The critic thereby becomes "a creative artist in miniature himself,"[52] since, just as the writer seeks to find incidents which crystallize his basic quality, so the critic seeks for "some conjuncture, some incident" in the work of the writer which condenses the writer's "universe of experience" into a dozen or so lines.

The condensation into a concrete verbal passage, or in Murry's term, "crystallization," is basic to style, whether in poetry or prose. In prose there is more emphasis on the intellectual and judicial, an emphasis which depends not only on the writer but on the taste of the age; but, otherwise, "the central problem of style," as it presents itself to the writer, is a question of "how shall he compel others to feel the particularity of his emotion?"[53] Or, to put the problem another way, "the essential quality of good writing is precision."[54] And, when we enquire as to the chief literary means of communicating precisely, the answer is in metaphor.

Metaphor, however, must be understood correctly. The ability to be metaphoric is not, as a rhetorician might explain it, merely the power to select appropriate images or pictorial illustrations—Murry thinks the visual image plays little part in metaphor—but rather the power to accumulate "perceptions of quality" with "their little fragments of context."[55] The metaphorical process in good writing, Murry thinks, is that "a perceived quality in one kind of existence is transferred to define a quality in another kind of existence."[56] The process, it might be noted, is—as usual with Murry—purposive and heightening.

He has no time (he observes, in what is no doubt an attack on the contemporary "imagists") for those concerned with the image for its own sake, "a pursuit that can only end in the artificialities of a new Euphuism."[57]

Since the image is a means to a common quality of life in various existences, it is not surprising that Murry goes a step further in the essay on "Metaphor" written in 1927[58] and views metaphor as a concomitant of transcendentalism: "However much we struggle, we cannot avoid transcendentalism, for we are seeking to approximate to a universe of quality with analogy for its most essential language through a universe of quantity with a language of identities. Sooner or later ..., a transcendentalism (which is only the name for a prodigious metaphor) is inevitable."[59] Such an approach helps to explain why, at this period, Murry's interests were turning to religion rather than to literature—though Murry, of course, would never allow an ultimate division here: "Religion and Literature are branches of the same everlasting root."[60]

In spite of the emphasis on "crystallization," the weakness in Murry's approach in *The Problem of Style* parallels the weakness in his form of Classicism: insufficient regard for *techne*. With his theory of metaphor as organic and progressive advancement from sensuous perception and intuition to a universal quality, all is seen from the "creative," even inspirational, side of writing. No help can be received from either the rhetorician or "man of taste." Murry holds the "low" view of rhetoric: "Rhetoric is the opposite of the process which I have called crystallization. Instead of condensing your emotion upon the cause, which becomes the symbol; instead of defining and making concrete your thought, by the aid of your sensuous perception; you give way to a mere verbal exaggeration of your feeling or your thought."[61] And he has little time for "good taste": "The most confusing of the many equivocations concealed in the word 'style' is that by which good taste in language is allowed to masquerade as a creative principle. Good taste in language will not carry a writer anywhere."[62]

What counts ultimately, for Murry, is genuineness of feeling and perception. And here perhaps is a deeper objection to his work, for such a view involves ultimately a judicial evaluation of feeling. Murry would reply that one does not judge another feeling so much as have a fellow-feeling of greatness. Yet the line between this and judgment or "taste" in feeling can be narrow. Murry's intuitions in matters of artistic value were in general sound—but not always. It is difficult not to judge him wrong in his depreciation of Yeats; his intuition did not sense the greatness in Yeats to the extent that, one feels, it should have done. And in admiring a book such as Doughty's *Travels in Arabia Deserta,* he has to allow that it is "artificial" in the best sense: "all good styles are achieved by artifice."[63] Although he covers himself by saying that the originating experience may "naturally" require a style composed by careful artifice, yet the fact remains that such a writer may—as Doughty did—make conscious use of many rhetorical devices.

To counteract Murry's theoretical overemphasis on *genuine* emotion one has to take into account the period in which he was living, one of *"empty* emotionalism," as Murry termed it.[64] He gives a picture of this in his novels[65] and refers to it in a number of his essays. His strong feeling against the prevailing atmosphere of the time and for the need for shock treatment is revealed in the following passage, in which he speaks of the "shallow literature of convention and fashion, created by superficial sensibilities, for the amusement of those many people who require from an author a reflection of their idle selves and satisfaction of their trivial appetites." Such people, he says, "want their literature soothing and narcotic and innocuous. 'How beautiful,' they murmur at their tea-parties, 'and what style!' Yet a glimpse of true beauty would frighten them out of their lives, and an inkling of the real nature of style would send their timorous minds squealing down the road to perdition."[66]

One is reminded of Wordsworth's attacks in his *Lyrical Ballads* preface on those "who talk of poetry as of a matter of amusement and idle pleasure; who will converse with us as gravely about a *taste* for poetry, as they express it, as if it were a thing as indifferent as a taste for rope-dancing, or Frontiniac or Sherry." Murry was performing at his period of literary history a task similar to Wordsworth's at his. At the same time, Murry's essay—like Wordsworth's—has lasting qualities. Most valuable, perhaps, are those passages in which precept is tied closely to example, particularly the illustrations taken from Shakespeare, such as the "subtlety of the orchestration" in Cleopatra's death scene.[67] It could be said of Murry, as Murry said of Coleridge, "So long as his attention could be fixed on a particular object, so long as he was engaged in deducing his general principles immediately from particular instances of the highest kind of poetic excellence, he was a critic indeed."[68]

CHAPTER 3

Discoveries of a Journalist-Critic

WHEN Murry began his career as a critic several years before World War I, the goals and standards suggested by the
terms "journalism" and "literary criticism" had much more in
common than they do now. Standing before J. A. Spender, the
editor of *The Westminster Gazette,* Murry could say with some
pride: "On that day I became what I have been ever since, a
professional journalist." At that period of history, Murry continues, one felt "that it was indeed no mean thing to be a journalist: that it was not a trade, but indeed a profession, with
precise and exacting standards of honour and integrity; and one
also felt the dignity of Liberalism."[1] Later, Murry paid tribute
to another editor; "as a literary critic I owe most," he said, to the
encouragement of Sir Bruce Richmond of *The Times Literary
Supplement.*[2]

The reasons for the widening gap between journalism and
criticism are not of concern here, and it may be that, on the
whole, the effects of the change have been favorable to criticism. Yet in one way there has been a distinct loss for the
average reader—or for the specialist reader who wants sometimes to relax in his reading. The journalist moves amongst
people, and he travels to discover what is of interest to his public. At its best, his lifework is distinguished by its humanity,
sense of adventure, and joy in discovery. These elements distinguish Murry's criticism. It would be difficult to read through
his essays—in collections appropriately entitled *Aspects of Literature, Countries of the Mind,* and *Discoveries*—without being
urged to look up at least some of the writers and works he introduces, or reintroduces, to the reader.

I *Theory Applied to Practice*

When Murry published his very confessional autobiography,
Between Two Worlds, in 1935, several critics based their reviews

on a comparison with Rousseau's *Confessions*—Murry usually emerging as a softer, more sentimental version of the French writer. Yet an examination of Murry's article "The Religion of Rousseau"[3] reveals a surprisingly rational-minded Rousseau, one who "sought to work out a logical foundation" for his insights into truth; he had to "translate these luminous convictions of his soul into arguments and conclusions." Here Murry expresses an understanding of Rousseau which sounds much like Murry himself, who was subject to feelings of certainty on which rational structures were built, only to be replaced later by other feelings of certainty and corresponding structures: "This unremitting endeavour to express an intuitive certainty in intellectual terms lies at the root of the many superficial contradictions in his work, and of the deeper contradiction which forms, as it were, the inward rhythm of his three great books. He seems to surge upwards on a passionate wave of revolutionary ideas, only to sink back into the calm of conservative or quietist conclusions."[4]

The main insight of Rousseau for Murry, that the idea of progress was an illusion, he discusses at greater length in *Heaven—and Earth*.[5] In his short early essay, really a review of a book entitled *La Formation Réligieuse de Jean-Jacques Rousseau*, he is concerned with the attitude and state of mind which caused Rousseau to think of man as basically good and free. That this concept has been interpreted into the easy and misleading notion of the "natural man," Murry sees as the fault of the critics, not the genius: the *mystique* has been degraded into *politique*—"they will read in the letter what was written in the spirit."[6]

In view of this attitude, we are less surprised than we might have been that this particular supporter of Rousseau ardently approved of Irving Babbitt's *Rousseau and Romanticism*, which is usually considered an attack on Rousseau. To Murry, Babbitt's book is "masterly"; it is of a kind "so rare that we are almost impelled to declare that it is the only book of modern criticism which can be compared for clarity and depth of thought with Mr. Santayana's *Three Philosophical Poets*."[7] It would be interesting to know whether Babbitt (who was, we might recall in passing, one of T. S. Eliot's respected teachers) would have welcomed Murry's support. It is true that, insofar as Murry's esthetic criticism was morally based, he is on Babbitt's side: "But this indictment [in *Rousseau and Romanticism*], it may be said by a modern critic, deals with morals, and we are discussing art and criticism. That the objection is conceivable is precisely the measure of our decadence. For the vital centre of our ethics is also the vital centre of our art."[8]

But then comes the difference from Babbitt's approach—Murry is a moralist via a Romantic appreciation of literature:

The values of literature, the standards by which it must be criticised, and the scheme according to which it must be arranged, are in the last resort moral. The sense that they should be more moral than morality affords no excuse for accepting them when they are less so. Literature should be a kingdom where a sterner morality, a more strenuous liberty prevails—where the artist may dispense if he will with the ethics of the society in which he lives, but only on condition of revealing a deeper insight into the moral law to whose allegiance man, in so far as he is man and not a beast, inevitably tends. Never, we suppose, was an age in which art stood in greater need of the true law of decorum than this.[9]

Similarly, although Murry approves of Babbitt's demand for a return to Aristotle, it means for Murry—as we have seen—an idealistic and even Romantically "Platonic" Aristotle. Like Babbitt, Murry is a humanist, even a Classical one: "Humanism must reassert itself. . . . The reassertion of humanism involves a recreation of a practical ideal of human life and conduct, and a strict subordination of the individual to this ideal. There must now be a period of critical and humanistic positivism in regard to ethics and to art."[10]

But, unlike Babbitt, Murry believes that the continuation of humanism demands a new consciousness of which Babbitt would almost certainly not approve: "We may say frankly that it is not to our elders that we think of applying for its rudiments. We regard them as no less misguided and a good deal less honest than ourselves. It is among our anarchists that we shall look most hopefully for our new traditionalists, if only because, in literature at least, they are more keenly aware of the nature of the abyss on the brink of which they are trembling."[11]

One might, in sum, say that Murry approves of the writer who is a humanist with the discipline of a Classicist but with the consciousness of a Romantic. Perhaps this attitude is, in practice, most clearly shown in his remarks about French writers. Baudelaire comes near his standards; but Victor Hugo fails because of lack of discipline; and Flaubert, because of cold formalism: "Had it not been that his Satanic defiance was moderated by a Satanic sense of *comme il faut,* Baudelaire might have gone the way of Victor Hugo and largely wasted his lesser genius in a mere fury of blowing."[12] Flaubert had not "the root of the matter in him. . . . Literature was to him an aesthetic revenge on life, not a culmination of it."[13] Baudelaire was "strong, masculine, deliberate, classical. . . . His affinities were with the disciplined and contemptuous romanticism of Stendhal and Mérimée."[14] It is notable that these three—Baudelaire, Stendhal, and Mérimée—had in common the ideal of "le Dandy." Murry gives an excellent account of dandyism,[15] and a good case could be made for his being "un Dandy" himself. Superficially, his record over his life suggests the intellectual playboy, leading people up certain paths, then turning on them for their stupidity; yet, as one studies and tries to understand Murry, one finds that all this is done with a strange inner integrity and sense of purpose.

That Murry admired both Rousseau and Babbitt suggests, as in other instances, that he needed a Classical bias in his theorists. For this reason, Gotthold Lessing was for Murry "probably the greatest literary critic we have had in Europe,"[16] and one wonders whether Murry saw in him a personal ideal. Lessing was an Aristotelian, but of Murry's kind: "It was the mind not the maxims of the master that fascinated him"[17]—a mind "so naturally comprehensive that it could, so to speak, begin anywhere." Lessing possessed the two great qualities of a critic—"a passion for clear distinction" and "a sense of the genetic and organic in things."[18]

Most of all, that which Murry admired and which perhaps helped to justify his own career, was the breadth of understanding that prevented Lessing from slipping into a narrow specialization. Lessing would find nothing amiss, if need be, to live in that realm which is labeled "literary criticism" and extend it into other disciplines: "Criticism, as Lessing understood and practiced it, was comprehensive and conscious of itself. It therefore passed continually into history, into philosophy and into religion."[19] This breadth of comprehension led him, like Murry, into journalism rather than the academic life.

Turning to English poetry, and leaving aside for the moment Murry's ideals of Keats and Shakespeare, we find that an English poet who met Murry's ideal of disciplined Romanticism was Thomas Hardy; and much credit should go to Murry for his ardent support of Hardy as poet. Hardy achieved a unity of technique and content, that harmony which Murry sought—a harmony of a different kind from that of the moralist or philosopher. Hardy is eminently successful in what Murry considers the two parts of the poetic process: one part, the "poetic method," is "the discovery of the symbol, the establishment of an equivalence." The other part is "an aesthetic apprehension of significance, the recognition of the all in the one." Hardy, says Murry, "stands high above all other modern poets by the deliberate purity of his responsiveness."[20]

Murry gives as one example of Hardy's excellence, "The Broken Appointment"—the poem beginning: "You did not come/And marching Time drew on, and wore me numb."—This "seeming fragment of personal experience," the disappointment of the lover, is intensified into a symbol with the overtones of a ruthless destiny: "the hopes not of a lover but of humanity are crushed beneath its rhythm."[21]

As he emphasized in *The Problem of Style,* Murry demanded precision of expression. He finds this quality in Hardy but not in Yeats. The forms and fantasies which crowd the mind of Yeats need "even for their own perfect embodiment, the discipline of the common perception."[22] Ultimately, he says in his review of the Yeats collection of poems entitled *The Wild Swans of Coole,* the poet is "empty" in that he has "the apparatus of enchantment, but no potency in his soul."[23] He lacks the "passionate apprehension" of Hardy. Yeats is an artist, Murry concludes, who allowed himself to drift into a dream, when he should, like Blake, have been "shaping" in the creative imagination.

The essays on Hardy and Yeats appeared in *The Athenaeum*

and were published with other comments on contemporary English authors in *Aspects of Literature* (1920). It is a good collection for appreciating the basis on which Murry evaluated and compared authors. For example, where Yeats, in comparison with Hardy, allowed himself to drift into vague dreaminess, Gerard Manley Hopkins is blamed for a formal rigidity which overwhelms sense, as well as for "a starvation of experience which his vocation imposed upon him."[24] This comment is a reflection more upon Murry's "experience" philosophy than upon Hopkins. In fairness to Murry, it must be allowed that he was among the first to recognize Hopkins' greatness in lyricism: "Musical elaboration is the chief characteristic of his work, and for this reason what seems to be the strangest of his experiments are his most essential achievement."[25] He must, however, "remain a poets' poet."[26] Later Murry seems to have had a higher opinion of the content of Hopkins' work: he refers to him as the "magician" between "the opposites of earthiness and ethereality."[27]

More universal in content, and a poet whom Murry places among the forefront of his contemporaries, is Edward Thomas, because his poetry has "the knowledge [which] should be the common property of the poetry of our time, marking it off from what went before and from what will come after."[28] Thus he was aware of the essential loneliness of modern man: "we may be, we are, the children of the universe; but we have 'neither father nor mother nor any playmate.' "[29] Thomas, though he was not great in that he never perfected his poetic means, had the stuff in him of great poetry, which, says Murry, "stands in this, that it expresses man's allegiance to his destiny." And although the "known truth" will vary from age to age, "the thrill of the recognition of the truth stands fast for all our human eternity."[30]

This knowledge of the truth of the age is what John Masefield lacks. Masefield has sought the "healing virtue where he believed it undefiled, in that miraculous English country whose magic ... is in Shakespeare, and whose strong rhythm is in Hardy."[31] But Masefield does not have an instinctive love of, so much as a conscious desire for, England. "The Georgians snatch at nature: they are never part of it. And there is some element of this desperation in Mr. Masefield"[32] in his attempt at the glorification of England. Murry never relaxed his demand for immediate sincerity in the experience of literature, in both content and expression—in fact, the two were united in the experience. Even if the subject matter did have the ring of "the truth of the age," Murry insisted that it should be artistically integrated. Samuel Butler's *The Way of All Flesh*, was, for Murry, a very unsatisfactory *roman à thèse*, in which Butler as "compère" is always egoistically present and trying "to replace the demonstration the narrative must afford, by arguments outside it."[33]

II *Some Lyrical Poets*

When all is said and done, it may well be that, apart from the work on Shakespeare and Keats, Murry's greatest contribution was to remind us of some of the minor treasures of English literature. His readable journalistic style, his aptitude for the familiar essay, his love of the English countryside, and his natural Romantic mysticism come together at their most relaxed and pleasant in his introductions to the poetry of John Clare[34] and the Countess of Winchelsea.[35] It is difficult to see how these essays could be improved, for all that was best in the amateur quality of Murry's criticism comes out in them. He describes the kind of nature-poet Clare was, conveying his beautiful simplicity:

The intensity with which he adored the country which he knew is without a parallel in English literature; of him it seems hardly a metaphor to say he was an actual part of his countryside. Away from it he pined; he became queer and irresponsible. With his plants and birds and bees and fields he was among his own people. The spiked thistle, the firetail, the hare, the white-nosed and the grandfather bee were his friends. Yet he hardly humanised them; he seems rather to have lived on the same level of existence as they, and to have known them as they know each other.[36]

Murry brings out the peculiarly naïve genius of Clare, referring, for example, to "the intense compression of a phrase like 'ploughed lands thin travelled by half-hungry sheep,' precise not merely to a fact, but to an emotion."[37] By comparison with the work of Keats and Wordsworth, Murry shows Clare's distinction and weakness: his achievement of unique "melody" rather than deep "harmony," the "emotional creation" which "leaps from particular to particular," lacking "that endorsement from a centre of disciplined experience which is the mark of the poetic imagination at its highest."[38] Clare was, it might be noticed in passing, of particular interest to Murry the farmer. He returns to the poet some thirty-five years later in an essay "Clare Revisited,"[39] and writes interestingly on Clare as the poet who sang of the evils of enclosure, the loss of freedom being symbolized by the enclosure of the old common lands, a loss which for Clare became the destruction of his vision.

In the volume in which "The Poetry of John Clare" appears, there are two other essays on lyrical poets, the nineteenth-century Clare coming between the eighteenth-century William Collins, and twentieth-century Walter de la Mare. Murry moved among poets to some extent as if they were all contemporaries, on a visit from a different era as from a different country, and not subject to the divisions common in academic study. In these three essays there is an interesting juxtaposition: the Romantic nature-child, Clare, is flanked by the style-conscious and over-aware Collins, whose sensibility was impoverished by concentration on the aesthetic, and by the modern de la Mare who seeks beauty in an anxious world.

For Murry, Collins was the prime example of the hyperconscious artist who "was prevented from feeling by the impatience of his intense desire to feel."[40] Only once, in the "Ode to Evening," did he achieve true style by transmuting a genuine experience into "the created thing." For the rest, he led himself astray by the very pursuit of style. "He was deficient," says Murry, "in the faculty of direct perception which best provides the material necessary if the technical process (even the most perfect) is not to operate idly, in the void; he was deficient in the vigour of mind essential to the fresh apprehension and memorable utterance of great commonplace."[41]

Murry also observes that two of Collins' best poems are school-boy poems, and these are "disturbing, for they show that the aesthetic impulse had reached the highest point of acuteness long before the sensibility could have established any real contact with experience at all."[42] Murry does not here pursue the problem of the relationship between aesthetic concentration and emotional experience, but returns to it in dealing with Spenser.[43] There are, incidentally, illustrations and asides in Murry's criticism which cannot be given credit in a summary. In the essay on Collins, for example, there is a revealing comparison of the treatment of the same scene by Collins, Gray, and Thomson.

It is interesting that Murry, who accused Yeats of drifting into dreams, should have applauded de la Mare for having "the courage of a dreamer." Although the poet treats of life haunted by death and decay, he remains dedicated to the beauty that disappears as soon as it is discerned: "In Mr. de la Mare's poetry we discover a trembling poise between the longing for an eternality of beauty and an acquiescence, an almost ecstatic acquiescence, in its transitoriness."[44] Murry makes some pertinent remarks on the dream as a modern literary theme and he quotes the last stanza of the poem "Dreams":

> What can a tired heart say,
> Which the wise of the world have made dumb?
> Save to the lonely dreams of a child,
>   "Return again, come!"

Commenting on this verse, Murry generalizes about dreams as basic to much of modern literature, in a way which, for example, could apply to the many characters of Eugene O'Neill who cannot bear to lose their "pipe-dreams":

To recognise that the dream is a dream, yet to refuse to put it away, this is the vital act of comprehension which animates the enduring part of the poetry of the present age. It is a reflection of our devastating experience and our shadowy faith; for even while we know that the dream is a dream, having no counterpart in the reality without us, it cannot be wholly surrendered because we live by its enchantment. For to live is to make ourselves of a certain quality, to fashion ourselves to a certain temper; and if the dream is impotent to reshape the stubborn world beyond us, its power to work upon our own souls is undiminished.[45]

At a period when Eliot and others were strongly in support of "the metaphysicals," Murry continued to favor the Spenserians. Some of his best essays are on the lyricists in the Spenser-Keats tradition, and in the essay on Spenser, "The Poets' Poet,"[46] he makes that poet the fount of English poetry, although he recognizes that Spenser is not popular and never will be in a democratic age. Spenser has not the right "interestingness." He is concerned little with themes, ideas, and emotions in the ordinary sense, but with form and beauty. Murry as critic could be getting himself into difficulties, since he attributed Collins' failure to an over-concentration on the aesthetic; but the difference is in the excessive strength of Spenser's *passion* for formal beauty: "we might put it that he could afford to run no risks by entertaining other emotions than those aroused by the pure pursuit of form and formal beauty."[47] The sense of beauty, says Murry, "did with Spenser precisely what it did with his pupil Keats, 'it obliterated all consideration.' "[48]

It is not surprising that Murry thinks little of the poetic achievement of the eighteenth century, which was essentially the century of "consideration." The "impassioned simplicity" which Murry thinks essential for the true lyric was missing; using the philosopher Ludwig Wittgenstein's "What can be shown, cannot be said" as support, Murry argues that the eighteenth century was afraid of the truths that were beyond reason, and therefore lyrical poetry was not possible in spite of the Neo-Classic arguments about the category of lyric as distinct from the epic or dramatic. Murry finds only five poets of the eighteenth century (before Blake) in whose poetry "there is something more than a fleeting glimpse of a reality beyond the actual"—Collins, Christopher Smart, Thomas Chatterton, William Cowper, Thomas Gray—and of these five "one killed himself, and three died melancholy-mad."[49] This charge of a Romantic critic against the eighteenth century is not new, but Murry's case is, as usual, well-put and interesting in its sidelights. For example, he admires Dr. Johnson, whom he sees as at war with himself, clinging the more closely to a naïve religious faith, the more he thunders against "the deserters of common sense."[50] Murry is particularly struck by Johnson's phrase "the hunger of the imagination which preys upon life" and by Johnson's defense of "Kit Smart," a poet, says Murry, who could glimpse a "simple and incredible purity."[51]

Murry, it might be said, only touches Samuel Johnson in passing and does not grapple with him in the way that modern
scholars do. It is true that, apart from Shakespeare, Keats, Lawrence, Blake, and Swift, Murry does not adequately deal with
the great figures of literature; but doing so is not his forte.
With an amateur sensibility, he fills in gaps which the learned
might leave; he reminds us that there were other literati around;
and, as he introduces us to them, they become people as well as
writers so that we want further acquaintance. In this way, he is
a kind critic. He does not, for example, dismiss Thomas Flatman as a failure because, as Flatman himself acknowledged, he
did not measure up to "Reverend Donne's and noble Herbert's
flame." Rather, Murry makes us want to know more about the
"failure": "in this, we think, lies the final and enduring interest
of Flatman. He is not a successful minor poet, nor an unsuccess-
ful one. He does not really belong to the race of minor poets
at all. He is a failure of a higher kind; and he is able constantly
to thrill us, even though we know we shall be disappointed,
with the expectation of some singular success."[52]

Most pleasing of all the essays about the minor poets is the
one on Anne Finch, Countess of Winchelsea, who was born
shortly after the Restoration. Murry is perfectly balanced in his
approach, which is both personal and textual; and he makes
us feel the genuine love and loveliness of the Countess' life and
the "sense of nuance" and "delicate emotional simplicity" of her
poetry, illustrated by just the right quotations. We catch a
glimpse of a whole society from a feminine point of view, but
one which had its effects on the greater life of the imagination,
as the inspiration to Pope's famous line springing from Anne's

> Nor will in fading silks compose
> Faintly the inimitable rose.
>
> Now the Jonquille o'ercomes the feeble brain;
> We faint beneath the aromatic pain.[53]

Incidentally, there is in the essay a picture of the ideal
English landed aristocracy, which suggests to us again that
Murry's real sympathies were with the old agricultural society
of England. He sees in Anne and her husband the perfect examples of a type

which, though it grows rarer, is assuredly not yet extinct in the English aristocracy: true ladies and true gentlemen who do not willingly provide paragraphs for the gossip-columns, nor take up postures innumerable in the illustrated weeklies: on their estates, in town, in the Royal Household itself, which they generally serve at some time in their lives, they live sequestered; secret charities, unpaid services, flow from them; and the love and honour of a countryside flows to them. Their felicity is enviable, but not envied, because they have deserved it: in word and deed, in courtesy and kindness, they remember that *noblesse oblige*.[54]

III *Some Prose Writers*

In criticizing prose, Murry turns mainly to the novel, but he appears to favor the French and even the Russian novel in translation to the English fiction. Even in English prose the prize seems to go not to a novelist but to Charles Doughty, the author of *Travels in Arabia Deserta* published in 1888: "no other book has been maintained on such a level for centuries."[55] In general, however, Murry takes the view that the best prose written in the first part of the nineteenth century was by the essayists and in the second part by the novelists. There are Macaulay and Carlyle but "both Macaulay and Carlyle represent the incursion of the imaginative realisation of the novelist into the dignified kingdom of history."[56] This imaginative incursion is justified, for the final purpose of the art of literature is "the power to awaken in the reader an intense and understanding contemplation of all that is."[57]

In this last phrase—"an understanding contemplation of all that is"—we realize that Murry is a particularly Classic critic when he considers the novel. He has the Aristotelian interest in an art which fuses philosophy and history. He demands a strong element of clarity and objectivity; and, in this connection, he quotes with approval Dr. Johnson's requirement that literature should be a just representation of human nature. Murry is critically bold enough—particularly courageous considering the period in which he was writing—to support the element of story in the novel: "A truly great novel is a tale to the simple, a parable to the wise, and a direct revelation of reality in the light of a unique consciousness to the man who has made it part of his being."[58]

Even in the didactic element of the novel, Murry is Classic. He allows that novels can entertain more than instruct—he gives *Robinson Crusoe* and *The Pickwick Papers* (Murry supported Dickens even when he was out of favor) as examples of his own favorites in entertainment—but he maintains (echoing Lawrence) that the kind of novels which were required at his particular period of history were thought-adventures, novels which might not be greatly enjoyable but which helped men on their way. He gives his own list of imaginative prose writers who helped him "up the mountain"—Plato, Stendhal, Dostoevsky, and Chekhov ("who is the great *artist* of the end"[59] and who summed up Western consciousness in a perfect reconciliation of the objective and the subjective). Novelists coming after Chekhov seem anticlimactic: he recognizes the genius of Proust and Joyce but he feels that they present nothing new. They only re-demonstrate that a stage of intellectual consciousness is ended: "What Tchehov had done sincerely and simply and perfectly, they were trying to do fashionably, elaborately and unnecessarily."[60]

He continues this theme in his essay, "The Break-up of the Novel." After H. G. Wells, Joseph Conrad, and Arnold Bennett and the "infinitely subtle craft" of Flaubert and Henry James, there is only Lawrence. He recognized the importance of Proust, Joyce, and Dorothy Richardson when their early works appeared in 1913–1914 and of their attempts to convey immediate consciousness untrammeled by any of the old conventions of the novelist; but he argues that extreme subjectivism leads only to an inartistic confusion. The new "subjectivist novelists seem to be chiefly moved by a desire to express the truth alone" whereas Chekhov and his English counterpart, Katherine Mansfield, "aim at an *art* which is compatible with the truth."[61] It is characteristic of Murry that he can recognize the genius of *Ulysses*, and his early support of Joyce is greatly to his credit; but, at the same time, he can find it wearying because Joyce refuses to meet "the common reality" and the compromise with a common, accepted language. Despite passages of great beauty, *Ulysses* as a whole must be considered "a gigantic aberration, a colossal waste of genius, the last extravagance of romanticism."[62]

The essay ends on an optimistic note, however, and suggests a development of the novel after the transitional "break-up" which subsequent events have tended to support. He notes Joyce's genius for comedy (*Ulysses* contains "at least one sustained passage of metaphysical comedy which justifies us in at least comparing his powers of intellectual imagination with those of Goethe and Dostoevsky") and suggests that "satirical Aristophanic comedy" is the literary resolution in an age of "exasperation."[63] He might have been predicting the "Lucky Jims" of Kingsley Amis and the comic satire of our "angry young men."

The great French and Russian writers obviously gave Murry something which the English did not. The effect of Dostoevsky and other Russian authors—and of "the Russian soul" in general—has been referred to.[64] The short essay on Stendhal reveals why the discovery of this writer was such an important element in Murry's life: Murry had found one who represented his own basic conflicts. "The reality of a man for Stendhal lay in his faculty of allowing all that is prudential and calculating in him to be swept aside by what is instinctive and passionate."[65] This statement could apply to Murry's lifelong battle, for, although he had said that he had made "Love all my Religion," he could never leave the world of analysis and anxiety—including financial concern over his personal circumstances, as perhaps nobody reared in the poor but careful suburbs of London can. This conflict between "the calculating" and "the all-giving" was interpreted by some as hypocrisy and became the basis, for example, of Aldous Huxley's caricature of him as Burlap in *Point Counterpoint.*

On the literary level there was also similarity between Murry and Stendhal. Stendhal falls between a self-styled Romanticism on a somewhat soulful level (*élan d'âme* was his expression for the passionate urge he admired) and a Classical clarity and concreteness, between *la force* and "analytical exposition." Stendhal, says Murry, comes between the Classic and Romantic; he is a tragic realist who—like Murry—naturally idolized Shakespeare since Shakespeare's tragic heroes play their part in the active life of a real world. But "tragic realism" meant more for Stendhal than an esthetic theory: "It was for him not merely the attitude of an artist towards life, not merely a philosophy which enabled the artist to express his vision of the truth and quality of life, it was also, and perhaps chiefly, a philosophy of conduct."[66]

To Stendhal, man had, in fact, not merely to suffer passively the blows of destiny; one's duty was to live out the tragic life: "The first thing was to be *une âme supérieure* (his beloved phrase), the second to assert it in act, the third—and a bad third—was to write about it."[67] One might see in this interpretation of Stendhal, Murry's own tendency to leave literature and criticism and to plunge into purposeful causes—only to plunge out again to get back to his pen. Murry shared something of the amateurishness and naïveté with which he associates Stendhal, qualities that come from being the follower rather than from being the original and the inventor for oneself. As Murry said, he had to have his heroes, and he had a long list of them; in much the same way, the novelist Stendhal was "less a creator of heroes, than a hero-worshipper."[68]

No doubt, much of Murry's love of French literature was due to an instinctive need to check the vaguer expressions arising from his English Romanticism. Such phrases as "that deeper style which lies beneath the words themselves"[69] are not devoid of meaning, but they do not lend themselves to amplification. For definitions he could build on, he looked to Remy de Gourmont and other French critics; and to restore his sense of logic and subtle enquiry he turned to "the wisdom of Anatole France" and to the psychological probing of Proust. Although Murry had said that there was nothing he could learn from Proust, this statement does not represent Murry's final appreciation of his work. Early in the publication of the parts of *À la Recherche du Temps Perdu*, Murry was extolling its greatness as "the subtlest of all modern psychological fictions,"[70] a brilliantly successful record of "the growth of a modern consciousness,"[71] a book sounding "the arrival of a new sensibility."[72] Despite a frequently "awkward complication" in the language—"Mr. Proust's language is sometimes alembicated to a point of grotesqueness"—the book has style because it has "at least one of the qualities of permanence, an animating soul."[73] Proust can be classed with Stendhal even: "we might more exactly apply to him a phrase which he himself has aptly used of a great predecessor, Stendhal, and say that his work has *la grande ossature du style*."[74]

One of Murry's strongest impulses was to put literary works into historical perspective, for he had a well-developed sense of *Zeitgeist*. Such an impulse may lead to "system-building" with its many attendant dangers, but it may also result in useful historical comparisons. One of the best of these occurs in the essay on Proust, whom Murry compares with another Frenchman who articulated a new sensibility, Rousseau:

To find an approximate parallel in the history of modern literature we should probably have to go back to Rousseau. There we should discover the paradox of a man not primarily a literary artist whose work revolutionised the literature of the next hundred years; M. Proust likewise is not primarily a literary artist. Nothing could be more significant than the length of the process of his finding his "invisible vocation." Like Rousseau, he is ultimately compelled to writing as a satisfaction for his sensibility. The chief point of difference is that where Rousseau was compelled to express his sensibility upon alien themes, M. Proust has been in the privileged position of one who could afford to wait for the truly inevitable occasion. Still, the only work of literature with which *À la Recherche du Temps Perdu* could profitably be compared is the *Confessions of Jean-Jacques*. There is a real likeness between the driving impulses at work in these books, and a careful comparison might enable us to determine the more important differences between the new sensibility of the eighteenth, and the new sensibility of the twentieth century. At all events, a century of science has passed between. M. Proust is not preoccupied with finding God, but with finding *la vraie vie*, though a previous quotation shows that where Rousseau always did, he sometimes does identify them. But more apparently still, a century of scientific psychology, of astronomical physics, of the biology of Natural Selection, has intervened. The last shreds of anthropocentrism have been worn away. Where Rousseau felt his own isolation and was tormented by the discrepancy between his dream and the reality, and could not reconcile himself to his isolation or his torment, M. Proust can. He accepts these conditions, he formulates them as an actual law of human existence; and the acceptance has been incorporated into the very mechanism of his sensibility. He discerns in the world that which he feels in himself; he is a Rousseau to whom some of the hidden causes of his perplexity have been made plain.[75]

The search for *la vraie vie* which Murry sees as animating Proust, animated Murry—in fact, Murry might be said to have used literature for just this purpose. He had a strong sense of what was "inside" and "outside" life. Rousseau and D. H. Lawrence were certainly "inside," they suffered "experience"—a word on which Murry built a whole "philosophy." He accepted the search for *la vraie vie* as a premise without feeling a need to define it, although it seems always to be associated with emotion, with anguish, and with the violent action which causes the extremes of feeling, with "alternate exaltation and catastrophe."[76]

Murry regards Anatole France as an example of the "renunciation of experience,"[77] the writer who paid this price for wisdom. For Murry, the distinction appears to be clear: "The chasm between living and being wise (which is to be *raisonnable*) is manifest. The condition of living is to be perpetually surprised, incessantly indignant or exultant, at what happens." Wisdom requires first that one stands apart from such involvement, and France is the man of wisdom who instinctively does so. Murry gives a good image of the relation of France and wisdom to the life-involved genius who experiences:

[France followed] a sequestered path, which ran equally by the side of the road of alternate exaltation and catastrophe which other men of equal genius must travel. Therefore he has seen men as it were in profile against the sky, but never face to face. Their runnings, their stumblings and their gesticulations are a tumultuous portion of the landscape rather than symbols of an intimate and personal possibility. They lend a baroque enchantment to the scene.[78]

France is not, in general, Murry's kind of writer; but he allows that such men of wisdom are necessary, if only to keep one on balance. One may have little in common with the thought of Anatole France, Murry says, "but it is sweet for us who inhabit his mind for a while. His touch is potent to soothe our fitful fevers."[79]

With the fairness Murry shows in dealing with a writer with whom he is little in sympathy, such as Anatole France, it comes as rather a shock to read Murry's violent reaction to Gustave Flaubert. It amounts to an attack on a writer who, according to

Murry, did not, like France, just stand apart from life; he "hated" life and accordingly "tried to persuade himself that the subject matter of a work of literature was of no account."[80] His work shows no "inner growth" since the "root of the matter" was not in him.[81] He spent years on "inwardly hollow" works such as *Salammbô, La Tentation,* and *Bouvard et Pécuchet*—a career which could be summed up as follows: "Literature was to him an ascetic revenge on life, not a culmination of it; he tore himself up by the roots and planted himself in the most highly artificial atmosphere which a considerable writer has ever breathed. Under this unhealthy stimulation he evolved for himself the doctrine of the sovereign autonomy of art."[82]

This "doctrine" is what Murry is really against. He saw it as a danger to the creative imagination and to the writing and appreciation of English literature. He was against, not so much Flaubert himself, as the current fashion of an idolized Flaubert as the leader of a mystique of "Art" divorced from *la vraie vie:* "the invention of 'Art' has done no good to art," Murry claimed.[83] In a later article, "Flaubert and Flaubart"[84] he refers to these followers of the arcane practice of "Art" as "Flaubartians"; and Murry then criticizes what he considers the precious and pointless verbal obscurity of E. E. Cummings and even Joyce. Such writing represents egocentric Rousseauism at its worst. The article, seen at a critical distance, is an unfair polemic; and, in a later edition of the collection in which it appears, Murry withdrew the essay. But this and similar polemics served their purpose in counterbalancing some of the extreme "esthetic" attitudes of the time.

In the original article on Flaubert, Murry's critical sense shows through. Flaubert's most individual achievement as a writer is, he thinks, in the "power of awakening in us a sense of the process of time,"[85] and he accepts that Flaubert is a master, "but he is a minor master. In the years he spent in perfecting the instrument he forgot ... what tunes are most worth playing."[86] Even so, there is a heroic side to Flaubert in his dedication to technique, even if it denied him genuine greatness: "Flaubert's work can never cease to smell of the lamp, but by the writing of one fine book and one perfect story, and his devoted researches into the capacity of language, he is one of the greatest minor heroes of letters."[87] Another compulsion of Flaubert which Murry considered dangerous was his association of the search for truth with "fantastic efforts of documentation."[88] Murry foresaw an age in which "fact-finding" would take the place of "truth-seeking," and he felt it necessary to restate the obvious truth that "the verisimilitude of art does not depend on documents"—and, indeed, neither does the "verisimilitude of history."[89]

The verisimilitude of art and history depends far less on documentation than on "the creative imagination and the sensibility from which the imagination is replenished."[90] Not that Murry did not think that the esthetic was all important—he did; but he did so in the way of Chekhov rather than Flaubert. For him Chekhov was almost the pure artist but, says Murry, "I do not wish to be understood as saying that Tchehov is a manifestation of *l'art pour l'art,* because in any commonly accepted sense of that phrase, he is not. Still, he might be considered as an exemplification of what the phrase might be made to mean."[91] The criterion for judging the true artist is the extent to which the artist discerns unity in multiplicity and manages to convey unity of esthetic impression—the greater the diversity of content and the more single the vision, the truer the artist. The majority of writers at one time represent; at another, they philosophize. They take an attitude to what they see. Chekhov does not do this—the unity he discovers has its own conviction. Murry several times refers to Chekhov's projected story about the serf "who squeezed the slave out of himself." Chekhov had done this and had achieved the freedom of a complete acceptance of life: life is indifferent, but man can forgive. Chekhov was an artist because, with a "simplicity" which was "very wise and very old" and which "completely under-cuts" the intellectual complexities of a Proust and Joyce,[92] he became conscious of a fundamental harmony. Life became a form of music to which one listened, and one experiences this music when listening to Chekhov.

In this theory one hears the "heavenly music" of Shelley, and Murry is aware of this fact (though the conception of a higher, or deeper, music and harmony which the artist mysteriously hears and makes audible to the reader is also fundamental to Milton, a poet to whom Murry gives less than due credit). In fact, Murry believes Tolstoy, Dostoevsky, and Chekhov to be the true successors of Wordsworth, Shelley, and Keats in their sense of pain and harmony, a sense illustrated by such passages as Keats's:

> None can usurp this height
> But those to whom the miseries of the world
> *Are* misery and will not let them rest

and Wordsworth's:

> When with an eye made quiet by the power
> Of harmony, and the deep power of joy
> We see into the life of things.[93]

Such considerations are far from the surface problems of technique, and nearer the concerns of religious ethos. And this is exactly what Murry considered great about Russian literature in that it caused literature again to deal seriously with "those elements in our nature ... which desire before all things to be good. Russian literature is absolutely permeated, saturated through and through, with a sense of the problem of conduct,"[94] a problem which is not just what shall a man do, but what shall a man believe. The separation, for example, of politics and religion could not occur in the Russian mind; "the temporal government of man was really only a symbol or parable of the spiritual."[95]

For Murry, obviously, criticism could not stay within narrow limits. That he was a genuine critic can surely not be doubted, although it is difficult to classify his criticism except by some vague term such as "creative criticism." It is not fair to dismiss it as "fictional," as "autobiographic," or as "poetic" criticism, as has been done; or it might be truer to say that Murry did write "fictional" criticism if this is understood to be, not untrue criticism, but criticism which employs the insight of the novelist. Murry could not invent as a true novelist—as Lawrence early pointed out and as his own attempts at the novel proved. But he could work creatively with the facts of history, especially literary history. And the result is a series of "critical portraits" which often make delightful reading and take us back with sympathy, if not agreement, to a man and his work. It is true of Jacques-Bénigne Bossuet, the seventeenth-century rhetorician and monument of Catholic orthodoxy, a man who on the surface is in every way the opposite to Murry but to whom Murry gives a grandeur and magnanimity, and even a living quality, persuading us that here is a man to be listened to.[96]

Nowhere, however, does Murry's peculiar synthesis, in which judicial criticism is enlivened by the sensibility of the novelist, show to better advantage than in the two essays on Henri Fredéric Amiel, the nineteenth-century Swiss author of a *Journal Intime*. Just as Murry rightly included the two essays on John Clare in his selection of early essays published in 1950, *John Clare and Other Studies,* so he was correct in including the two on Amiel. Amiel is presented on several levels: there is the sense, which we always get with Murry, of the critic really having grappled with his work and of presenting a central aspect, well supported by quotations. The essay on Amiel is a model of this form.

With his historical sense, Murry makes Amiel a symbol of the nineteenth century: Amiel is torn between belief in a personal god and in the accumulating scientific evidence of an apparently indifferent universe, and he fails to find a third way. "With his intellect he accepted the universe of science, with his heart he admitted the necessity of religion and morality.... He sounded in his soul the whole octave of the nineteenth century consciousness."[97] He was a microcosm of the moral perturbation of the period, a learned man—a professor of esthetics and philosophy—who, with profound intellectual introspection, argued himself into despair, and who, in trying to achieve perfection, became a "perfectionist" who died of *la maladie de l'idéal.*

No doubt Amiel can be labeled as "timid" and as "afraid of life," especially in his long love affair, yet as Murry says, "it needed nothing less than a hero to make so ruthless a record of his own timidities."[98] As Murry observes, he is almost the opposite of the giants of the period; but he is invaluable in helping us understand what the giants overcame. Moreover, after reading Murry's criticism and cultural comment, there lingers a sense of having witnessed a tragedy. While keeping to his subject, Murry has given Amiel stature and has made us sympathize with his downfall. One wonders whether Murry could, after all, have been a successful novelist and playwright if he had, like his beloved Shakespeare, taken more from history.

CHAPTER 4

The Keatsian Critic

FOR Murry, Shakespeare was the ideal and Keats was the way. Such a brief summary sounds suspect, yet there is truth in its very simplicity. Murry accepted Shakespeare simply and without qualification as supreme; it was natural for him to state at the end of an illuminating analytic study of Shakespeare's plays that "Shakespeare's dream is God's and Shakespeare God's dream."[1] When Murry first attempted to compose lectures on Shakespeare, he found he could not approach his ideal directly. Keats, however, provided the perfect intermediary: "I saw that my one chance of making intelligible those slowly formed convictions of mine concerning Shakespeare was to use the greatest of his successors, John Keats, as though he were a mediator between the normal consciousness of men and the pure poetic consciousness in which form alone Shakespeare remains to us."[2]

The importance of Shakespeare and Keats for Murry was not confined to literature—it permeated his whole existence. In the autobiographical work, *Between Two Words,* Shakespeare—together with an ideal yeoman farmer—"is England." Little else is said of Shakespeare, but Keats becomes the inspiring guide. Murry describes the emotional, even physical, upheaval he experienced when he chanced in 1917 upon Sir Sidney Colvin's *Life of Keats,* and read extracts from the letters and *The Fall of Hyperion* with a new understanding—"it was the voice of Truth, speaking from the tomb." A way of life had begun: "The barriers were down. Though it might take me a lifetime to explore the world of human feeling and thought before me, the gate at least was open, and I had entered in."[3]

Throughout his lifetime of "explorative experience," Murry made touchstones of certain remarks by Keats, referring to them constantly. Few books, whatever the subject, would not include some quotations such as: "Call this world if you please 'The vale of Soul-making' "; "I am certain of nothing but of the Holiness of the heart's affections and the truth of imagination"; "A man's life of any worth is a continual allegory. . . . Shakespeare led a life of Allegory: his works are the comments on it"; "We never really understand fine things until we have gone the same steps as the author." Murry, in fact, found in the young lyric poet words which expressed his own emotional attitude and even his method of work. As Keats was the poet who strove for the generous state of "Negative Capability,"* Murry tried to be the corresponding critic.

There were close similarities, too, in the actual experiences of the two writers—in the love affairs and in the caring for beloved relatives who were sick and tubercular. No doubt such personal identification had its dangers for the critic, and Murry did not altogether escape them. At the same time, the seriousness of the association and the passionate sincerity of Murry are transmitted to the reader; it is easy to understand why *Keats and Shakespeare* (1926) has been the most popular of his books of criticism. In some ways, it is the ideal introduction to a poet, as many undergraduates can testify; it is not an abstract of the "main points" of a poet's literary career, as introductions tend to be, but the spirited presentation of a genius who, as man and artist, is a warm and living reality for the critic writing about him.

At the same time, it must be admitted that a popular and enthusiastic presentation does not necessarily make the book sound literary criticism. In fact, the mature scholar is apt to resent the attitude of total revelation, one in which the author throws the reader a challenge but implies that it would be in bad taste to pick up the glove. Bonamy Dobrée notes this "hands off John Keats" approach in his original review of *Keats and Shakespeare*,[4] and David Daiches strikes the same chord in his more recent review of *Keats:* "Mr. Murry approaches Keats with passionate and devoted sympathy and with an almost proprietary attitude, as though he alone, as a result of some profound fellow-feeling, had penetrated to the depths of Keats's personality and genius."[5]

* See below, p. 83.

But neither critic can dismiss Murry lightly. Professor Dobrée goes on to assert, "It is an illuminating, deeply pondered study, and, whatever its faults may be, there is no book on Keats I would rather possess and keep by me on my shelves." We might turn to yet a third respected scholar who finds himself torn in his appreciation of Murry's work; E. M. W. Tillyard, indeed, gives the ultimate in summaries: "Mr. Middleton Murry's *Keats and Shakespeare* is at once the best and the worst book on Keats."[6]

Probably, on first approach, it is best to accept the book as it is, without trying to classify it. Then, if the reader wishes to abstract from it a "purer" form of literary criticism—as modern critics are now doing—he will not go unrewarded.

I *Soul Journey of Genius*

In his *Study of Keats's Poetic Life,* as he subtitles the book, Murry follows the basic pattern he had developed in his earlier book on Dostoevsky, so that, although the book has the progress of a personal biography, its landmarks are the works of the artist. One might say that Murry reads the poems into the life rather than the life into the poems. His book has the interest of a narrative, but just as the chronological events are the poems, so the conflicts are less with other people than with other poetic attitudes, such as those represented by Wordsworth and Milton. Keats endures the trials of the "Vale of Soul-Making" until, at the end of the astonishing four years of his poetic career, he "is with Shakespeare." Keats's "most intimate history," Murry observes, "could be written in terms of his rejection first of Wordsworth, then of Milton in favour of a deeper and unchanging loyalty to Shakespeare."[7]

Keats starts his soul journey, according to Murry, in 1816 with *Sleep and Poetry* in which the poet speaks of the "vast idea" before him; and in *Endymion,* in the following year, he begins "proving [it] upon the pulses." What was the "vast idea" of Keats? With its post-rational apprehension of the union of beauty and truth (Murry could never understand why Keats's famous identification has caused so much controversy), Murry's definition echoes the Romanticism he outlined in his debate with T. S. Eliot: Keats saw "that the rational faculty was impotent to achieve truth, that intuitive apprehension was the sole faculty by which an ultimate truth could be known, that this truth could be recognised for what it was only by its beauty, that perceptions of beauty were premonitions of a finer reality, that the way towards intuitive knowledge of this reality lay through a reverence for the instinctive impulses, and that somehow in this final knowledge all discords would be reconciled."[8]

Murry balances his generalizations with more specific insights. An example is his understanding of the way in which Keats, at this time, was being influenced by Shakespeare. Keats was reading *King Lear* while relaxing at a seaside resort on the Isle of Wight, and wrote a "Sonnet on the Sea." Keats, as he himself observes in one of his letters, was haunted by Edgar's remark to Gloucester, "Hark! do you hear the sea?" Murry shows, mainly by reference to the letters, that—although the only visible connections between Keats's sonnet and Shakespeare is the use of the word "eye-balls"—the words of Edgar's description of the cliff and sea were "running verbatim in his mind." The "eternal whispering," used by Keats to describe the sea, was equally applicable to the words of *King Lear;* therefore, "the sea and Shakespeare had become, at a moment of intense receptivity, part of the same thought for Keats."[9]

It is at this time also that Keats is working through Wordsworth and expressing his objection to "the Wordsworthian or egotistical sublime." Wordsworth is becoming "comfortable"; in "The Gypsies," for example, there is no "search after truth." Wordsworth, in fact, had allowed himself to be betrayed, says Murry, into "an intellectual self-consciousness" and away from the "natural and spontaneous self-awareness" and the "loyalty to the instinctive impulses" which Shakespeare exemplified. Keats had what Wordsworth had lost, an immediate "genuineness of being." That is to say, Murry goes on, "if we read the story of Keats loyally, we come into possession of a truth such that the old and vexing conflicts between art and morality, between literature and life, cease to exist for us. Pure poetry . . . is revealed to us as the natural utterance of the finest and completest living."[10]

Keats has reached a spiritual state which he terms "Negative Capability," which was to be an important—perhaps the most important—phrase in Murry's life. It becomes extended into a religious ideal, the state which Christ attained: "it is more than tolerance, it is forgiveness." Murry uses the word "acceptance," that is, "a forgiveness which forgives not only men but life itself, not only the pains which men inflict, but the pains which are knit up in the very nature of existence."[11] Later, in an essay on "Keats and Milton," Murry goes so far as to say: "The Negative Capability of the poet achieves its natural consummation in the humility of the Christian before the Cross."[12] One sees why Murry was just as ready to write a book on Christ as on Keats, and on God as on Shakespeare. He tried to achieve the state of "Negative Capability," in criticism and in life, to be receptively open to all that was most important to man, to partake of a sort of mystical all-roundedness. For him, "True philosophy is precisely that Negative Capability that was so supremely manifested in Shakespeare. It proceeds from a natural submission of the self to all experience."[13]

This philosophy of being wide-open to all experience which Murry developed, helped to make him a good critic and editor, but it was less certain as a guide to conduct. He tried to explain and take over what he understood as Keats's idea of knowledge —a knowledge which is "essentially self-engendered; it is the self's creation of itself out of experience."[14] How successful Murry was in developing for his own purposes the philosophy of a young lyrical poet is an interesting question. Perhaps the basic tension in Murry sprang from this desire for full and open experience on the one hand, and, on the other, from a strong urge to find a permanent order (evident, for example, in his constant attempts to define the true society).

It may be because of such a basic tension that Murry is particularly concerned with Keats's power to transcend contradictions. Thus in 1818, Keats, as he endured the dying of his beloved brother Tom, was learning that life was a bitter contradiction—"on the one hand its beauty, on the other its pain." When he yearns to transcend this by maturing to the state of "High reason, and the love of good and ill,"[15] he discovers this ideal in reading *King Lear*—"that example of the intensity of contemplation which 'makes all disagreeables evaporate from their being in close relationship with Beauty and Truth.' "[16]

Keats, Murry says, was developing to a point "beyond all rebellion." "I have," Keats said, "loved the principle of beauty in
all things," which Murry concludes, with considerable evidence,
should be read not as "I have loved the principle of beauty—in
all things" but as "I have loved the principle—of beauty in all
things."[17] Unfortunately, Keats did not live long enough to put
that love into full effect—to realize, as Murry is sure he would
have done, the dramatic power of his genius "to reveal to men
that good and ill are to be loved; not only the faculty to see that
the sum of things is supremely beautiful, but the faculty to show
to other men that it is supremely beautiful."[18]

Murry insists upon a complete acceptance of the towering
greatness of Keats before any attempt is made to analyze him.
Thus he is "amazed, then indignant" when he reads in a *Life of
Keats* that "there was a great spiritual flaw in his nature."[19] By
what measurement can one say that, he demands; and he accuses the biographer of "the old trick of average humanity when
it is confronted with genius; it takes from it what it can com-
fortably accommodate, and throws the rest away as nothing
worth."[20] At the other extreme, however, Murry does not altogether avoid the excesses of hagiography. How far, for example,
can any poet be "greater than his actual achievement"? And it
is perhaps an escape from definition to speak of Keats's "depth
of thought, not discursive thought, but the poetic thought that
lies beneath 'the mighty abstract idea of Beauty in all things.' "[21]
It is true that in an addendum Murry tries to cover the objection,
making a comment on his own method as well as on the use of
the intellectual in Keats. The passage should in fairness be
quoted:

There may be some who will demur to my declaring, *sans phrase,* that
"the ambition of my intellect" [quoted from a letter by Keats] has
nothing to do with discursive thought. I can well imagine the temp-
tation of the sceptical critic to turn on me with: "Mr. Murry insists
that Keats means what he says, but when Keats says something that
does not fit with Mr. Murry's theory, he has no compunction in declaring that Keats means the very opposite of what he says." I am
afraid that the very nature of my attempt in this book makes it impossible to safeguard myself against such criticism, and I am certain

that there are many other passages in my narrative which are open to the same attack.

In general I would say this—and the grounds of my assertion are implicit in my whole narrative—Keats means what he says always when he is being a pure poet. When he is using the language of discourse he cannot always mean what he says, for the simple reason that he cannot always say what he means. He has to use words that were not made for his purposes. Just as his "philosophy" is almost the direct opposite of philosophy in the ordinary sense, so here "intellectual" ambition is unintellectual. If authority for such an interpretation is required, I should refer to such a passage as this (24th September 1819: to George):

"The only means of strengthening one's intellect is to make up one's mind about nothing—to let the mind be a thoroughfare for all thoughts, not a select party."

That is to say for Keats the only means of strengthening the intellect is what the rationalist would consider a complete abnegation of intellect.

I believe that I could produce similar authority for every interpretation of Keats that I have made. I have not attempted to do so, not so much because it would make an already difficult narrative more cumbersome, as because my story of Keats will stand or fall on other grounds than these.[22]

Perhaps one answer to this is that, even if the young poet is consistent, Murry himself is not consistent: if such "poetic thought" leads only to poetry, the end justifies the means; but Murry tries to make it lead to arguable conclusions.

At the end of 1818 two events occurred which, observes Murry, were climactic in Keats's "soul-journey"—the death of his brother Tom and the meeting with Fanny Brawne. Keats entitled the first *Hyperion* "A Fragment," but Murry maintains it is a complete poem. The main character of the poem, or the character on whom the poem turns, is Apollo, the immortal poet, who according to Murry is equivalent eventually to Keats. But Apollo cannot come into the poem until the end since most of it was written during Tom's illness when Keats deliberately turned away from life (a reason for Keats's use of Miltonics at this period, since Milton was "a man of genius in abstraction from the torment of experience."[23])

But, when Tom died and the ordeal and sacrifice were over, "the gates of life are flung wide for Keats."[24] He falls in love (Murry parallels these events with quotations from *Hyperion*), and in the third book Mnemosyne enters—more than memory, the new order, "the vast idea," or as Murry says, "Being itself, made conscious." With this consciousness, Keats had finished *becoming* a great poet: "Nothing remains for him but to *be* a great poet."[25] With this assurance, he enters his *annus mirabilis,* the year 1819, assured in poetry and in love. He writes the "poems of delighted happiness," "Ever Let the Fancy Roam" and "The Eve of St. Agnes" with "its opulent sensuous confidence ... the brief dayspring of Keats's passion translated into terms of the poetic imagination."[26]

But the ecstacy of love was soon to give way to the ecstacy of despair. Because of poverty and the nearness of death, "he was on the brink of that 'dying into life' which was to be endured by Apollo as the condition of his full divinity."[27] But despair was accompanied by a new "disinterestedness," the painful but elevating discovery "that things must be as they are." Murry compares the Keats of 1819 with the Keats of 1818: "The contrast is between Keats the spontaneous and unconscious poet; and Keats the conscious, yet still spontaneous poet. And this is the great poet: the poet who remains loyal to his own spontaneous poetic nature when he confronts the burden of the mystery, who knows by a secret sign that beauty is in all things and that in that beauty is there truth, who cannot rest until he has discovered it. Such a great poet Keats had now become."[28]

Because of this approach—and this often justifies Murry's method for, although we may not like the preliminary scaffolding, the results can be striking—Murry is able to develop a convincing explanation of the sonnet beginning "Why did I laugh tonight?" and ending "Death is Life's high meed," a sonnet which is "the conquering of a despair by a deeper faith." Such conquering involves great sacrifice. In "La Belle Dame sans Merci," La Belle Dame is Fanny Brawne; but "she is also the beauty of life itself which is claiming, through Fanny, Keats for its sacrifice and victim."[29] Keats has reached the stage of Hamlet, that "unembittered irony of the soul which begins to see beyond its pain,"[30] that acceptance of human destiny which is "a yea-saying to the sum of things," that ultimate comprehension of human life in which "beauty is truth and truth beauty." Murry sees no difficulty in this last observation. He resents the famous words being "pitifully misunderstood as the utterance of a sort of aestheticism." The Grecian Urn does not merely give delight to the senses; it is the "symbol and prophecy of a comprehension of human life to which mankind can attain." It is the culmination of a soul journey, the realization that "the truth of human life was beautiful, and that its truth was its beauty."[31]

In Chapter x, Murry expands on this development of soul. It is an important chapter both as an essay in understanding Keats' famous "Vale of Soul-Making" letter and also as an exposition of the premises of Murry's attitude to life. Toward the end of his life Murry was to reaffirm the fundamental and decisive influence that this letter had on him. It enabled him to accept the fullness of experience, to endure and be enriched by it.[32] He became convinced of two kinds of knowledge, the "poetic process" leading to soul knowledge and the rational process leading to mind knowledge. In approaching the mystery of life, "what is a simple act of apprehension for soul-knowledge is a complicated and impossible one for mind-knowledge." And "in the realm of soul knowledge the tiniest gleam, loyally followed, flames slowly into full comprehension; but the most arduous and subtle efforts of mind knowledge to enter that realm end only in confusion and bitterness."[33]

There is then a distinct cleavage between these two forms of knowledge. The "central axiom" of all poetic thought is that "reality is harmonious," whereas rational thought assumes that reality is rational. There is, Murry would admit, a strong element of mysticism in his understanding of the forms of knowledge; he quotes parallel passages from Meister Eckhart. Soul-knowledge develops from a union of conscious and unconscious knowledge in which the mind is subordinated to and in harmony with instinctive being, when, as Keats says, the Heart is "the Mind's Bible." It is in the nature of such knowledge that it must derive from personal experience—it cannot be merely speculative: "Do you not see how necessary a world of Pains and Troubles is to school an Intelligence and make it a Soul?" cries Keats.

Murry, claiming, with supporting evidence, that this is Keats's view, extends the idea still further: "Soul-knowledge is God-knowledge." Keats, says Murry, "seriously thinks that the system of soul-making he has apprehended is the fundamental and essential religious truth, of which all religions are partial and simplified statements."[34] In this, there is a "final knowledge" echoed in "that is all/Ye know on earth, and all ye need to know." At this point, the question for Keats was not achieving victory—this he had achieved—so much as consolidating it.

Before Murry goes on to this last stage of Keats's journey, he gives a strong plea for poetry as a way to revelation and prophecy. The poet for Murry is the *vates sacer;* he cannot be reduced to terms of rationalism or estheticism: "I believe, for I have found it so by experience, that pure poetry contains a revelation, and I would far rather stand for the ancients in their belief that the poet is directly inspired by God than with the moderns in theirs that the poet is a *lusus naturae.*"[35] Murry begs that we should "take great poetry seriously"—even the church must; for the church has lost a reality. This reality is twofold :"It is a knowledge of the unity and harmony of the universe which can be reached only through the individual's knowledge of unity and harmony in himself. This two-fold knowledge is achieved by the pure poet,"[36] of whom the two greatest examples are, of course, Keats and Shakespeare. To some extent, Murry may be understood as extending the views of Matthew Arnold, who was, early in Murry's career, the champion of critics; although where Arnold was, if we may speak broadly, replacing religion with culture, Murry was trying to re-achieve religion through the culture of the poets.

By April 1819, Keats had "won a great victory" in the achievement of his "complete individuality"; and, by the end of May, he had written the *Odes.* But circumstances were against him; he needed money and forced himself to do some hack writing with the unromantic Charles Brown, and he was becoming increasingly aware of the impossibility of consummating his love affair with Fanny Brawne. As a relief from his hack work, Keats wrote *Lamia,* which Murry describes as "imaginative autobiography ... of the most exact and faithful kind. Keats is Lycius, Fanny Brawne is the Lamia, and Apollonius is Charles Brown, the realist, trying to break Fanny's spell over Keats by insisting upon her as a female animal."[37] This interpretation enables Murry to answer the objection, raised by Sir Sidney Colvin and others, that the reader is asked to sympathize with the serpentine enchantress and to side against the friendly sage. The one undeniable fact is that Keats was in love with Lamia. " 'I like Fanny Brawne and cannot help it,' addressed to Charles Brown, is the key to *Lamia*."38

At this period, Keats is turning to Milton again and away from Shakespeare; and this change is for Murry a sign of escape into abstractionism. (There is—unintentionally—a suggestion, at this point in Murry's narrative, that Milton and Shakespeare vie for Keats's soul somewhat as the good and evil angels do for Faust's.) In Keats's letters, as well as in his reworking of *Hyperion,* he directs his interest to Milton at the same time that he tries not to think about Fanny. But, as misfortunes pile up, he achieves miraculously a pleasure in his loneliness and writes the severe, beautiful "Ode to Autumn." He abandons "the sin of uttering soul-knowledge through an effort of mind-knowledge";39 he finally gives up the Miltonics of *Hyperion:* "Shakespeare had triumphed in Keats's soul."40

Such a brief summary of the main movement of Murry's book cannot do justice to the incidental expositions, such as the skillful explanation of the second *Hyperion,* in which Murry continues his earlier interpretation: the poet now "passes beyond the conception of the death into life which is undergone by Apollo in the final book of the first *Hyperion*." He becomes aware of what it is "to die and live again before his fated hour."41 Even if one does not agree with Murry about this difficult poem, with its symbolism of Thea, Saturn, and Moneta, and on many other points of textual interpretation, one has to allow that he has opened the way for fruitful discussion—as succeeding critics have illustrated.

Murry is convinced that Keats was on his way to being a great playwright. He never wrote the plays he dreamed of because, Murry believes, of the torments that arose from his love for Fanny Brawne and destroyed him. Murry strongly emphasizes the effect of this love, admonishing those who feel that Keats overhumiliated himself: "those who cannot understand Keats's love, will never understand his poetry, for these two things spring from a single source."42 Although, in a later essay, Murry recants completely his harsh judgment on Fanny in the light of more recent research, his main argument is not affected; what killed Keats was not Fanny so much as separation from her.

II *The Wisdom of Keats*

Besides a number of articles in various periodicals, Murry wrote one more book on Keats, consisting of a collection of essays several times revised: it appeared first as *Studies in Keats* (1930), then as *Studies in Keats: New and Old* (1939), as *The Mystery of Keats* (1949), and as *Keats* (1955). All the essays amplified his general attempt, as he said, "to reveal a little more of what I have called—following Keats himself—the *prophetic* element in his work and life: the continual presence in himself of the power whose workings he discerned in Shakespeare, when he said, 'Shakespeare led a life of Allegory: his works are the comment on it.' "[43]

In the last version, *Keats,* almost the entire first half is devoted to Keats's relation to three women: Fanny Brawne, Fanny Keats, and Isabella Jones. Fanny Brawne, as mentioned earlier, is completely reinstated in Murry's favor. The essay fills sixty pages, emphasizing her integrity and the honesty of her feeling in her letters to Fanny Keats and to Charles Brown when he wanted permission to publish a letter and some poems that involved her. There follows a pleasant biographical essay on Fanny Keats and a forceful refutation of Robert Gittings' thesis that the "Bright Star" sonnet was written not about Fanny Brawne but about Mrs. Isabella Jones. Of the other essays, several amplify comments Murry made in *Keats and Shakespeare;* or they reply to objections from other Keats critics.

Some of these essays constitute a reply in themselves to critics who accused Murry of not going beyond a loose impressionism. He could be very exact in the best tradition of *exposition de texte.* In the essay "The Realms of Gold," for example, he examines the sonnet "On First Looking into Chapman's Homer" and comments on "the imagery and emotion of eager exploration" in the octave and "the imagery and emotion of breathless discovery" in the sestet. He focuses his power of analysis and his impressionistic insight in a revealing study of the poem, demonstrating how it is "the final harmonious ordering" of a whole series of ideas and experiences in Keats's life and work—his thoughts about nature, his response to the first sight of the ocean, his own "vast idea" of poetry to come. Murry gives examples from Keats's early and inferior verse to show how the ideas began and matured into the words of the famous sonnet. Thus Murry gives the lines from one of Keats's first ventures, "I stood tiptoe upon a little hill": "Or by the moon lifting her silver rim/Above a cloud, and with a gradual swim/Coming into the blue with all her light." "There, unmistakably," observes Murry, "is the naive and charming bud of the full-flavoured: 'Then felt I like some watcher of the skies/When a new planet *swims* into his ken.'" The changing of "moon" to "new planet," the association with a new ocean, the historical detail of Cortez from Keats's schoolboy reading of Robertson's *America* (although this source has been contested)—these and other details are blended into the organic whole of the sonnet.[44]

Murry does not change his basic attitude in the essays but explores problems that he has been turning over in his mind, such as the meaning of the lines, "Truth the best music in a first-born song" and "The feel of *not* to feel it" as well as Keats's use of the word "speculation." Also, he makes of Keats a center from which to explore and evaluate the rest of life; in three essays he examines Keats in relation to Milton, Wordsworth, and Blake; and in another he explores what Keats has to say on friendship. Elsewhere he has essays on "Keats and Coleridge" and "Keats and Shelley," and in the course of other works he refers to Keats in relation to Thomas Chatterton, George Gissing, Lawrence, Mansfield, Leo Tolstoy, Albert Schweitzer, and Christ.

At the same time, the reader is struck by the number of times Murry returns to Milton in these essays—almost compulsively, as if he has to resolve for himself his own relationship to Milton. The battle in *Keats and Shakespeare* between Shakespeare and Milton for Keats's soul has been noted. In the essay "Keats and Coleridge," which is in the form of an imaginary conversation, the two poets discuss Milton at some length and agree that, of English poets, Milton has the greatest style and probably even the greatest character; but Shakespeare, because he possesses "the true idea of love," is superior in being without one definite style and character; "Milton's identity seems stamped on every line, Shakespeare's seems to have uttered *itself*." Milton's "egotism is truly sublime," but it is egotism, and must be struggled against.[45] Keats and Blake, in the essay entitled "Keats and Blake," had "one remarkable thing in common. They both came to a realisation of their own truth by way of a struggle with Milton."[46]

Again in "Keats and Wordsworth," Murry finds a starting point in Milton. He suggests that Keats in *Hyperion* was "caught between a desire for Miltonic objectivity and a compulsion towards Wordsworthian subjectivity," or between "the Miltonic ideal and Wordsworthian necessity." Part of Keats's struggle was "to consider Wordsworth's genius, and how he differs from Milton." Although Wordsworth had more affinity with Milton than with Shakespeare, he was close in spirit to Keats, to whom Milton was "remote." "In the essential," Murry believed, "Wordsworth and Keats were at one concerning the nature of the love which is the source of 'the vision and the faculty divine'.... For both of them the essential character of this love was that it was 'self-destroying.'" To prove his point Murry quotes from *The Excursion,* showing some distinct echoes in Keats, a close one being Keats's "Mute! Yet I can read/A wondrous lesson in thy silver face" echoing "And in their silver faces could he read Unutterable love" and "And in the silence of his face I read/His overflowing spirit."

Although Keats was disturbed by Wordsworth's pride and egotism in actual life, the influence of Wordsworth on his poetry, says Murry, was subtle and pervasive. Keats felt at home with the "imaginative feeling" of Wordsworth. In the use of Classical mythology, Wordsworth conveyed for Keats the right "feeling-tone" or "sensation." "I will say at a venture that Milton's classicism is still in the main a medieval classicism that sees through a glass darkly and not face to face. Wordsworth's classicism is that of an emancipated soul who has inherited the intellectual freedom to see things in a pagan clarity, at the very moment that it is laying anew the foundations of the Christian religion. Greek myth is a legend for Milton, for Wordsworth a vision." And Keats was destined to pursue this vision in a way that Wordsworth had not done.[47]

It is not surprising that Milton scholars disagreed. In *The Miltonic Setting,* E. M. W. Tillyard complains that Murry had contributed to the critical depreciation of Milton. In one of the most suggestive criticisms of Murry's work, Dr. Tillyard explains why he regards *Keats and Shakespeare* as "at once the best and worst book on Keats." It is best because "no other critic has studied Keats with so fierce a concentration, with such sustained sympathy. Poems, unheeded or slurred over by others, have come alive in Mr. Murry's mind; letters, hitherto slackly read, have yielded up to him their immediate significance and their place in the trend of Keats's mental growth." But the study is a worst one because "Keats is made the victim of a larger theory. ... he must be attached to a certain human type of excellence, of which Shakespeare is the most eminent English example ... and any competing attractions are in the last resort Sirens, Cyclopses, or Lotus-Eaters.... Mr. Murry makes Milton the Cyclops of Keats's Odyssey."[48]

Replying in his essay "Keats and Milton," Murry sees two issues: first, the right estimate of Milton, and Murry admits that he is inclined to underestimate Milton; and, second, the role Milton played in Keats's development. Murry maintains his position about Milton's significance for Keats, and takes issue with Dr. Tillyard's comment that "Mr. Murry really must not be allowed to confine the great generalities of human feeling to the kind of man he happens to prefer; and if Keats's problem and its solution grew out of the 'torment of experience,' so too did Milton's." The key to the difference, says Murry, is in Tillyard's term, the great *generalities* of feeling; for what Murry was concerned to elucidate in Keats was precisely a great *particularity* of feeling.[49] Logically, Murry's answer is dubious, since he himself stresses the general appeal of Keats: to Keats's "moments of victory belongs the poetry which is a possession forever of the human soul in its pilgrimage."[50] What really bothers Murry, being the kind of critic he is, is the difference in "feeling-type." He is at home with Keats and Shakespeare, "the Catholic feeling-type"; he is alien to Milton, "the Protestant feeling-type." Although Murry probably becomes too broad in his classification, the terms are suggestive. The Catholic type stresses the Incarnation and is naturally sacramental; the Protestant stresses the Atonement and is naturally exegetic. The Protestant too has a proud sense of election—thus Milton's "astonishing con-

fidence in human reason, and primarily in his own reason."
Milton was "naturally full of his rather magnificent Self,"
whereas Keats was "naturally self-less."[51] Although Keats was
not, like Milton, a profound Christian, he had the true humility of Christ. Milton's theology was that of an "amazingly gifted
undergraduate"—in fact, by his theology, he emancipated himself from Christianity.[52]

Murry, indeed, is more than "inclined to underestimate Milton"; he resents him. Perhaps the main reason for this resent-
ment is implied in the last paragraph of the essay. Murry la-
ments that a poet "so evidently great, in some valid sense of the
word, so magnificent an artist of poetry, should have so little
intimate meaning for us. We cannot make him real. He does
not, either in his great effects or his little ones, touch our depths.
He demonstrates, but he never reveals. He describes beauty
beautifully; but truth never becomes beauty at his touch."[53]
Milton refuses intimacy, and a sense of intimacy with writers
was both the strength and weakness of Murry's form of criticism.

There are disagreements on other aspects of Keats, including,
of course, the meaning of "Beauty is Truth...," which Murry
makes the title of one of his essays. He summarizes other critical
judgments on the last two lines of "The Ode on a Grecian Urn":
"For Doctor Bridges the final lines redeemed a poor poem; for
Mr. Eliot they spoil a good one; for Sir Arthur Quiller-Couch
they are ignorant and uneducated; for Mr. Richards that still
ambiguous unity he calls 'a pseudo-statement.' "[54] (In a note
Murry acknowledges that "pseudo-statement" is not used by
Richards in a derogatory manner.) Murry's complaint against
these approaches is that they are based too directly on a mental
analysis. We have to identify intuitively with the process by
which Keats arrived at his statement, and then perhaps his meaning becomes evident :"We do not have to ask, coldly, what is the
meaning of 'Beauty is Truth.' We have to ask what meaning it
could possibly bear to such a man at such a moment in order to
assuage his pain. Again, we have to ask this as men to whom
bitter experience is not alien and remote."[55]

If Murry could have stopped there, his guess at the way to understand the mysterious words of Keats would have been as good
as anybody else's. But, as he so often does, he feels urged to go

beyond—to try to define that which, according to him, can only be subjectively arrived at: "We know that words which contain a message of peace in moments such as Keats was then enduring will not be easy words. They may be simple, but they will not be easy.... Such a message is in the words: 'Not my will, but Thine be done'.... It is meaning of this kind, and of this order, that we must seek in 'Beauty is Truth, Truth Beauty,' if we are ever to know what they meant to Keats or what Keats meant by them."[56]

When Murry goes still further, we find passages which, if they were all, would justify his opponents' charges against him of windy rhetoric: "The Truth—the true Truth—is such that it awakens Love, and the Truth that awakens Love is Beautiful";[57] and "Beauty is Truth, Truth Beauty. What Keats is saying is profoundly true, and it is profoundly beautiful. Nor would it be profoundly beautiful if it were not profoundly true. So much is surely obvious. But equally, it would not be profoundly true, if it were not profoundly beautiful."[58]

Yet Murry cannot be entirely blamed for writing in a fashion in which his personal feelings come to the surface; in one way or another, such prose was in the atmosphere of the 1920's and 1930's. There is, for example, a marked difference between the reaction to Murry of other critics of this period—in such publications as Ernest de Selincourt's edition of the *Poems of John Keats* (1926), F. R. Leavis' *"Keats"* (1936), and Dorothy Hewlett's *Adonais: A Life of John Keats* (1938)—and the reaction of critics of recent years in, for example, E. C. Pettet's *On the Poetry of Keats* (1957), W. J. Bate's *John Keats* (1963), and Aileen Ward's *John Keats: The Making of a Poet* (1963).

In the earlier group there is the tension of battle. De Selincourt observes that "Mr. Murry's argument here [some disputed lines of *The Fall of Hyperion*] as elsewhere, is vitiated by his acceptance of what Keats says when it suits his theory, and rejecting it when Keats has the temerity to differ from him."[59] (Murry's answer to this attack was a carefully documented essay, "The Poet and the Dreamer."[60]) For Leavis, Keats's genius "is not really illuminated by the procedure of *Keats and Shakespeare*, or, except as another of Metabiology's cloudy trophies, exalted."[61] Dorothy Hewlett is, interestingly, apparently ironic about Murry's mysticism—"The retreat into the 'Cave of Solitude' Mr. Middleton Murry (*Studies in Keats*) claims as a mystic experience, but few of us have the gift or power of mysticism to follow him into those hidden regions of the spirit"—but her own interpretation of the same passage sounds remarkably like Murry in rhapsodic mood: "My own interpretation is that Endymion, alone and forlorn, had to gather together the shattered pieces of his life and in pain of spirit withdraw into himself and there find himself.... He had lost himself and now he must withdraw into the fastnesses of his own being to find himself, to gain that inner control which alone enables a human being to give himself wholly and completely in love; the love that is stronger than death."[62]

The critics of the last decade write on another plane: The tone is much more relaxed emotionally; the comments are more exact and professional; and the orientation is to the text. Murry's points are taken as they are, apart from the subjective growth in which they developed, often being placed in footnotes, such as: "Murry reads something into Keats's argument of which the text gives no hint if the disputed passage [187–210 of the Introduction to *The Fall of Hyperion*] is dropped, as he recommends: that Keats counted himself 'a true poet,' one who had 'utterly rejected dreams,' and thus exempt from Moneta's condemnation (*Keats*, p. 242). Keats may have cancelled the disputed passage, not because he disagreed with Moneta's condemnation (which remains in 11. 166–70)...,"[63] and "Reynolds' review is that erroneously assigned by Murry to Hayden."[64] There is a cautious, judicial evaluation in place of the enthusiasm and "discipleship": "though Middleton Murry sometimes over-states his case with an unnecessary denigration of Milton, he is almost certainly right in his sustained contention that Milton and the composition of *Hyperion* deflected Keats from the course of his own native genius";[65] "Middleton Murry is probably right in his suggestion that the inflowing warmth and rapture of the opening of Book III [of *Hyperion*] owes something to the awakening of his love for Fanny Brawne";[66] and "Murry is probably right in his repeated contention that Keats wanted 188–210 [of the Induction to *The Fall of Hyperion*] deleted. But he is quite wrong in asserting that the lines 'conflict with

the real argument of the poem' (*The Mystery of Keats,* p. 192).
The passage is consistent with the rest of the Induction. . . ."[67]

Murry continued to refer to Keats in his later books, but in
a manner which was almost completely opposed to the general
trend of criticism. In *Adam and Eve* (1944), a book examining
the true "man-woman relationship," Keats's life story is presented as a parable of Christian love : "The disappointment by
disease and death of his passionate love, with its magical combination of ideal and real, of spiritual and physical, is one of
the most poignant stories of human suffering that I know. It is
scarcely less than a crucifixion, and, like the Crucifixion, it
awakens in us thoughts beyond the reaches of our souls."[68]
Keats had become canonized in Murry's mind, not only as the
poet next to Shakespeare, but as a great religious teacher. It is
not surprising that a long comparison of Keats with Albert
Schweitzer comes to the conclusion: "I believe that on the question of ethics itself Keats is right and Schweitzer wrong."[69] In
the same year that this book appeared, Lord Gorell published
his *John Keats: The Principle of Beauty,* in which he took Murry to task for being too solemn about Keats, and for not accepting
the pleasures of his poetry as such.[70] But Murry could not take
his heroes lightly.

CHAPTER 5

The Englishness of Murry

THE person who is determined to leave himself open to a wealth of experience and sensation often has as strong an urge to organize his experiences into a purposeful system. To the person himself this systemizing will probably seem a progress toward unity, a harmonious integration of a chaos of thoughts and feelings; but an outsider is equally apt to consider the "system" as an articulation of what was there to begin with. By an extraordinary path, the experiencer reaches the ordinary; he suffers the abnormal painfully, until he achieves his "norm."

Murry's goal was—if it may be so described without any note of deprecation—to be a "normal Englishman." With the help of Keats, Blake, Lawrence, and Christ, he eventually found his way to the normal. He wrote in his journal a few years before his death: "There is, indeed, no doubt at all that, in the last resort, art to me is nothing in comparison—with what shall I call it? My own 'personal happiness' gives the wrong slant. What could have made me endure the abject personal misery I endured from 1932–1939? My own personal reconciliation with life, much rather. And by life I mean the normal conditions of human existence: being married, having children, providing for them."[1]

The particular quality of being "English" did not mean, of course, narrow nationalism to Murry: his view was—as he expressed it in *Community Farm*, also a late work—that "England's first duty to the world society is to be England as it is France's to be France."[2] Indeed, his love of Greek and Latin and French literature helped him to distinguish the English Romantic quality about which he argued with T. S. Eliot and which he found in Chaucer, Shakespeare, Keats, and Hardy—a group whom he considered in particular to be "deeply native to the English soil and the English soul."[3] (Perhaps his most serious charge against Milton was that he wrote in a "foreign idiom.") Murry had to explore Christian humanist culture in which "Englishness" was rooted, and he had to say more about the man who was for him the perfect Englishman—Shakespeare. He undertakes these tasks in *Heaven—and Earth* and in *Shakespeare*. Of the two authors who have written at length about Murry, Mr. Lea claims that *Heaven—and Earth* is Murry's most important work; Mr. Mairet, *Shakespeare*.

Of the twenty-six chapters of *Heaven—and Earth*, eighteen are given to Englishmen—to Chaucer, Shakespeare, Cromwell, Milton, Godwin, Wordsworth, Shelley, and Morris—and the remaining eight to Montaigne, Rousseau, Goethe, and Marx. (In the American edition, the title was changed to *Heroes of Thought*, and a foreword connected England with New England and introduced the names of Roger Williams and Lincoln.) Such vast surveys are not critically popular in the 1960's, but few would deny that a general sense of cultural tradition is necessary for any scholar. One critic has suggested that it would be an excellent college book; it gives a perspective within which to place the individual work, and it sets one arguing, pro or con, in the mainstream of Western culture and literature. Since the book itself is a form of summary, only an indication of the main direction of Murry's thought is attempted here.

I *The Heroic Pattern*

The cycle of history which this book, *Heaven—and Earth*, represents starts with Chaucer. The salient fact for Murry is that Chaucer knew an order and peace which was destroyed by the institution which should have implemented it—the Church. Chaucer is the "sanest" and also the "wisest" of England's great poets, because the order into which he was born was of divine origin. Its great social unit was the village community, seen at its best with the poor Christ-like parson. But there were the hunting monks, the money-grabbing friars, the corrupt "somnours" and "pardoners" which the Church allowed to be parasitic. Therefore, the Church lost the compulsive power of universal spiritual authority which Murry considers essential. Not that we can ever go back to an old form; but we can learn, and Murry suggests useful lessons based on the betrayal of the landed peasant, the illusion of a purely legal freedom, and the moral rights involved in "holding" and "owning" land.

With Montaigne comes what Murry calls "the birth of the individual," though it was in a profound sense an unselfish individualism :"To have turned his power of self-forgetfulness upon himself—this was Montaigne's triumph. He looked upon the Self with the eyes of the not-Self.... His book is one long and infinitely various act of self-discovery, self-objectification, made possible only by self-forgetfulness."⁴ In this self-knowledge, combined with the liberation of the individual, Montaigne is, says Murry, the complement of Shakespeare. His essays and Shakespeare's plays are "personal obverse and impersonal reverse of a single medal that imperishably commemorates the inward spirit of the high Renaissance in Europe. It is, in my eyes, far from an accident that in *The Tempest* Shakespeare turns to Montaigne for help in his great and final argument for Forgiveness."⁵

After the failure of the Church as a universal order, there was a period of disorder, then a new period of order under Elizabeth, but of secular order. Shakespeare's strong sense of, and desire for, order is expressed in many passages: Murry quotes from *Richard II* and the famous speech of Ulysses in *Troilus and Cressida*. In *King Lear*, the tragedy, says Murry, is irresponsible kingship: "The fount of Order betrays the principle of Order." Cordelia answered as she did, in a way which may seem "more than a little cold" to the modern mind, because she, unlike her father, clung to the principle—she loved "according to her bond."⁶ By this approach Shakespeare gives depth also to *Romeo and Juliet;* the loyalty to family order creates a much stronger tension with personal desire than is possible in modern times.

But there is another order which Murry finds in Shakespeare, an order of the imagination, in which for a time in the theater as in the old Catholic Church "heaven and earth meet naturally together." The imagination, as Murry understands it, is very closely related to religion: "Religion is still the simplest and most universal speech of Imagination, and the attitude of Imagination is humility, real humility, an emptying of one's self in order that a greater power may take posssession."⁷ This religious enlargement exists in Shakespeare, "the knowledge that Order is much more than uniformity, and that the One foundation of all reality is revealed in the richness of all the infinite variety of these things as they simply are."[8] In a sense, Shakespeare brings the old Catholic idea and the individualism of Montaigne into an organic whole. When the visible universal church was shattered, "Shakespeare created its universality anew, in the selfless imagination of an individual man."[9]

Unfortunately we, in turn, have today lost this order of Shakespeare. The reason, says Murry, is—the machine. We have lost the organic life, "the vital harmony." Somehow the task of civilization today—and especially that of the artist—is to rediscover this order while incorporating the machine. Men have to do this by a supreme and conscious effort of the imagination, "an imaginative understanding of Change becoming an understanding change of Imagination. . . . Imagination is the consciousness of creative Life."[10] Because Murry cannot limit "creative Life" to any particular form, and because the current situation is so closely-knit and urgent, he feels that the artist should have the widest concern in enlarging human consciousness. Today the choice is between consciousness or "bestial Oblivion," and "Art helps to create Oblivion if it is informed by anything less than a complete awareness of the situation of Humanity today."[11]

As in the case of Carlyle, one of Murry's heroes is Cromwell; and, like Carlyle, Murry finds a literary quality in Cromwell's speeches. Cromwell understood the necessity of order, the fundamental order of the union of earthly and divine, which Murry found in the medieval Catholic Church and in Shakespeare; but Cromwell failed in implementing the military theocracy which would have allowed religious equality—equality before God. Moreover, he had one quality which Milton had not and which made him ultimately a greater man than Milton: he could be "tender to the weakness of men." This element is lacking even in the *Areopagitica*—for which Murry "would give all *Paradise Lost*." The latter "may be Art; but this is Prophecy—wherein the Artist forgets himself, and speaks at once for God and a People."[12]

This is the same charge from a different angle that Murry in his *Keats and Shakespeare* makes against Milton. Milton would never have "Negative Capability" because his God was an intellectual part of himself, not a God of love. Murry allows that this criticism could sound too simple, even "childish," but he claims that Keats and Blake both make this lack of love the main point of their criticism of Milton. Blake after his well-known inversion of God and Satan in *The Marriage of Heaven and Hell,* imagines, in *Milton,* Milton's redemption by the power of love. But, as Milton existed in history, there was "something inhuman" about him. In a chapter typically entitled "Lear without Cordelia," Murry finds that this inhumanity is clearly apparent in the contrast between *The Tempest* and *Samson Agonistes,* when, for example, the final meditation of Prospero with its statement "the rarer action is/In virtue than in vengeance," is compared with the words of Manoa after the death of Samson:

> on his enemies
> Fully reveng'd, hath left them years of mourning,
> And lamentation to the sons of *Caphtor*
> Through all *Philistian* bounds.

With that sentiment of revenge and death at the end, Murry feels "that the majesty of poetry has been prostituted and degraded."[13] Milton, in fact, despite his religious profession and despite his great genius and power to liberate intellectually, was not a great Christian.

It is noticeable that Murry skips the great figures of eighteenth-century Classicism, going from Milton to three thinkers who created the European culture of the nineteenth century. Later he was to do a biography of Swift, a writer who was "the very antipodes" of himself,[14] though probably less so than Murry realized. But in the scheme of a developing Christian civilization, Murry sees the next step, after the Cromwellian period, in Rousseau, Goethe, and Godwin. Unfortunately, although these thinkers were able to glimpse in various ways the right path, they were less effective in guiding people along it. Some who did start along it, like Wordsworth and Coleridge, drew back in later years.

Rousseau's great original insight was that the "Idea of Progress"—as it was then understood by the élite and as it is still understood by many today in spite of twentieth-century history—was an illusion since there could be no civilized advance without moral progress; and "it was essential to the Idea of Progress that moral progress was automatic, since the Idea of Progress was none other than the idea that every advance in mechanical and material Civilisation was self-evidently an advance for humanity." Rousseau saw clearly, long before the suffering of war and other evils forced others to see it, that "under an advancing material civilisation, unless society becomes a moral entity, it becomes a madhouse."[15]

There are, says Murry, only two moral systems: "the divine right of kings" and authority derived from the people. Under the second, which is the accepted form in the modern world, sovereignty resides in the "general will"—which it is vital to distinguish from "the will of all." The great political question which Rousseau sought to answer was how to achieve the true "general will." Basically, "What Rousseau was absolutely clear about was that the achievement of a true society depended on an unremitting moral effort on the part of its members, on their being permeated by the understanding that the health of the whole depended on the health of every individual part. A true society was a society determined to overcome all inertia, and the symbol of this determination was the new and sacramental understanding of "the social contract"[16]—where "community [would] become the reality of communion."[17]

Society, then, was conscious and moral and symbolic of a larger union. It was sacramental. Murry saw in Goethe what he calls "the new sacramentalism." The "gradual turning of himself from the subjectively to the objectively romantic ... he rightly regarded as his great achievement."[18] Influenced by Shakespeare and Spinoza, Goethe became vividly and simultaneously aware of the phenomenon and its significance. "The supreme thing," Murry quotes Goethe, "would be to comprehend that everything actual is in itself theoretical.... We must not try to get behind phenomena—they themselves are the lesson"—to which, as a parallel, Murry quotes Blake's "To see a world in a grain of sand."[19] However, to see things with this simple but profound clarity is a rare gift, one possessed by the creative spirit or "daemonic man." Murry defines "daemonic" as the "creative power of Nature manifest on the specifically human level."[20] Goethe is the prophet of this power of nature becoming manifest in human history, which Murry sees as a process of which the consummation will be an order governed by Christian love. He quotes Goethe: "we shall all advance gradually from a Christianity of word and creed to a Christianity of feeling and act."[21] It is an optimistic and easy thing to say, but it is the only hope, avers Murry. But such understanding must be implemented by suffering, the *price* of experience; and this Goethe lacked.

Murry admits that Godwin is a lesser figure, but one to whom justice has not been done. It is easy to mock the lack of "realism" in his idea of "universal benevolence," and his failure to take into account economic factors in determining society. Yet his naïve idealism can be a corrective to the equally naïve belief that economic growth will lead to the millennium. Godwin believed that "the ideal was also a motive in the process of historical 'necessity,' and ultimately the most enduring motive of all."[22]

In spite of great suffering, Godwin clung to his vision of an ideal society. Other Romantics did not, notably Wordsworth, with whom Murry next deals. He compares the very different development of Blake and Wordsworth after the first flush of enthusiasm at the outbreak of the French Revolution. Murry feels particularly bitter about Wordsworth, perhaps because there is some parallel between them in that they represent a similar "Englishness." Wordsworth to a much greater extent than his famous contemporaries had roots: "the integrity of feeling to which he had trusted was deeply rooted in a spot of English soil, and in its way of life."[23] He found an approximation to the true ideal of human society in his own country-folk of the Dales. When he utterly opposed the abstractions of revolutionary idealism and of commercialism, he produced his great patriotic poems. Then he changed; he became a timid reactionary, deploring any kind of change; when he could have been a great poet of a land of liberty.

In particular—and here Murry returns to his own conception of the social order based on the village of Chaucer's day—he supported the abuse of pluralism in a corrupt Church by which "men without piety nor learning, were allowed to accumulate benefices in their hands, and put in starved curates to do their work,"[24] a new form of the old crime of the Church against the village. In giving a cause for the decline in Wordsworth's poetry and outlook, which began about 1805–1807, Murry thinks that there might have been a connection with his suppression of the Annette Vallon affair. Be that as it may, "Wordsworth slowly descended from a faith in an ideal England to servile acquiescence in a corrupt reality in the name of Christianity," but "Blake steadily struggled upward, in complete isolation, to a more and more sublime vision of his own country as the place where, as in a type, the redemption of mankind by the Divine Humanity of Jesus would be begun." This vision is epitomized in the famous verses beginning "And did those feet in ancient time/Walk upon England's mountains green?" which "have come more and more to be felt as the voice of the living soul of Christian England."[25]

What of the next generation of Romantics? There is no question about Keats, already amply dealt with as next to Shakespeare. With Shelley, Murry opposes the "ineffectual angel" view of this poet. Shelley came when the village community was finally being destroyed and *private* property had become a rational but inhuman concept in the primary necessities of life. Shelley did not just follow Godwin in repudiating this new concept. He was naturally idealistic, believing in social revolution; but he was also *realistically* aware that "before equality of possessions comes to be in a democratic society, there will have to be a majority of people who *believe* in such equality as a moral or religious truth."[26] In supporting his statements, Murry quotes some of the inspired passages from "Hellas," "The Ode to Liberty," and other poems.

Shelley was in the tradition of the English anti-absolutist revolutionaries of the seventeenth century, which left as its "ideal legacy" the annihilation of the concept of divine right of kings. There were two other anti-absolutist revolutions—the French, which left as *its* ideal legacy "a second nullification of the divine right of Kings, and (more important) the assertion of equal political rights of all men as men"—and then the Russian, also a "nullification of the divine right of Kings, but, more important, the assertion of equal economic rights for all men as men."[27]

But there were basic differences between the Rousseauistic

and Marxist visions: where Rousseau saw the rational Idea of Progress as an illusion, Marx accepted it as a material reality. Yet Murry sees the Marxist salvation as one based on despair, since Marx, because of historical factors in Germany, de-emphasized the moral and political evolution of society. There was a tremendous bias in Marx's thought—"a constantly operative unconscious tendency to minimise the efficacy and the necessity of the moral motive in history."[28] And there is a difference between Rousseau and Marx which Murry thinks important: the former can be understood by the simple mind, the latter cannot; for Marx does violence to the simple mind, "our deep, instinctive sense of ultimate right and wrong."[29]

Finally, as a climax—though it may seem after the illustrious names that have gone by, an anti-climax—comes William Morris. It does not matter too much whether William Morris seems anti-climactic as artist and thinker, since it is as a symbol that Murry uses Morris to come full circle: "What was in Chaucer's age the actuality has become for Morris the ideal."[30] Morris saw fourteenth-century Gothic in a new way; he saw the great churches built not by the priests but by the working men: "the service of God lay in the creative fulfillment of man."[31] Morris —like Murry at this time—saw art as the expression of social life; genuine popular art was possible in the Chaucerian Gothic period, but it was not possible in the period in which Morris lived. For the sake of art, he was willing to forego his art and to prepare for the society out of which art would grow naturally. English poetry of the first order had ended with Keats. Now was necessary a new *kind* of life, an "elemental social regeneration," the positive complement to Marx's "final demonstration of the inevitability of social catastrophe under capitalist industrialism."[32] Morris and Marx between them, in fact, effected "the twin realizations of the central prophecy of Rousseau"[33]—that society would not be regenerated without intense moral and spiritual effort on the part of its members. Both men were "possessed by the historical vision"; but, where Marx read history through economics, Morris read history through art. And where Marx worked through theory, Morris worked through experience. Morris, in fact, had "the genius of experiencing." As a result he looked back to, and tried to recreate in living terms, the state in which "religious communion and natural community were in harmony."[34]

It is true that Murry's political views changed after the publication of *Heaven—and Earth*. He gave up party Socialism, but only because it did not serve his ideal of a small religious-centered community on the land—of the neo-medieval village living, as it were, in the spirit of Chaucer and William Morris. He tried the practical experiment in community living which he records in *Community Farm*. Since his social goal was to a large extent a personal, an even subjective, ideal, he found, in later years, that he could come close to achieving it in the actual spot of England where he was living. After all, he *was* living in the land of his major literary heroes, his domestic life was happily settled, and he was a communicant at the village church. He had achieved an integration of personal and social order, of which the supreme expression was to be found in the work of Shakespeare. Though *Shakespeare* was published two years before *Heaven—and Earth,* it was Shakespeare, like Keats, who was the life-long study.

II *Shakespeare*

Murry could not write about Shakespeare without somehow "knowing him" personally, even intimately. He admits in his *Shakespeare* that he does not have much historical evidence to support him, but he feels obliged to put in order what clues he has: "It is on such twigs as these that I propose to spin my theory of Shakespeare's career up to the writing of *Hamlet*. That it is no more than a theory, I am as conscious as anybody. But that it is necessary to have a theory I know by experience."[35]

From the scholarly point of view, Murry's is a dangerous approach, of which the following may serve as an example. Murry refers to the "image-sensation" which developed from Shakespeare's apparent association of fawning flattery with spaniels receiving sweetmeats from nobles, in the complex images involving "spaniel-fawning" and "the candied tongue [licking] absurd pomp" which appear in *Julius Caesar, Hamlet,* and *Antony and Cleopatra*. Obviously the basic image of hounds under the table eating tidbits thrown to them by Elizabethan diners corresponds with something vivid and disgusting in

Shakespeare's mind. Murry traces this disgust to a decisive moment in the young Shakespeare's life, his being called before Sir Thomas Lucy for stealing deer in Lucy's park.

"I am persuaded," says Murry, "that I can enter into the actual 'sensation' which Shakespeare experienced when he stood before Sir Thomas Lucy in Charlecote Hall." The occasion made "an indelible impression on his unconscious mind" as Shakespeare "was standing before the table in an Elizabethan hall, watching the hounds wagging their tails, licking the hands of a pompous company, gobbling up the rich and sticky sweetmeats thrown to them—and this experience so deeply nauseated Shakespeare that it went on working unconsciously within him, and became a self-creating image of servility and flattery."[36] It is an appealingly dramatic picture, but it called forth the following admonition:

Quite apart from the fact that the tale about Shakespeare's deer-stealing in Lucy's park is a manifest fiction—Sir Thomas Lucy had no deer-park at Charlecote when Shakespeare was a boy—this kind of speculative reconstruction, by which a set of linked images is assumed without any evidence to have originated in a specific incident, is illegitimate. The device is as seductive to the imaginative writer as it is attractive to a public agog to know what Shakespeare chose not to tell. Cluster [image-cluster] criticism provides a means whereby we may in some measure draw aside the veil shrouding Shakespeare's personality, but if associative linkages are to become the subject of unthrifty inference the truth which they reveal will be submerged in a sea of specious error.[37]

Sometimes Murry's intuitive insights had a luckier fate, one being his deduction from an elaborate simile of housebuilding in *Henry IV, Part II* that Shakespeare was, about 1598, engaged in building or renovating a house for himself, a fact which has been historically confirmed in his purchase in 1597 of the New Place, which stood in great need of repair.[38] Murry's insights, too, lead to important themes, such as the character which develops from the Bastard in *King John,* on which E. M. W. Tillyard has remarked: "Middleton Murry has written so well of the Bastard's character and of the new vein of creation that went to his making that I need treat of him only as embodying Shakespeare's political opinions."[39]

Murry was aware of the "hit or miss" nature of his approach, but he persevered. His reward is that he achieves, and communicates, an organic fullness in his appreciation of Shakespeare, so that, whether or not we have to check the factual truth of some of his conclusions, we can hardly fail—as several critics have pointed out—to finish the book without an enlarged understanding of Shakespeare. Certainly, as the publishing history of the book proves, it has been a most popular introduction. The reviewer in *The Times Literary Supplement* had this to say: "From beginning to end the book is rich in ideas and observation which will notably help the plain man to see more of the beauty and the meaning of his plays."[40] And Murry could have received no greater compliment than that he was the critic for "the plain man."

At the same time, Murry's work has had an effect on Shakespeare scholarship, the most direct effect perhaps being on G. Wilson Knight. "When after leaving Oxford I was groping for a way to express what I had to say about Shakespeare, Middleton Murry's articles in the monthly *Adelphi* magazine acted on me like an avatar," Knight wrote in a recent essay;[41] and he has acknowledged both his debt to Murry's "general approach and militant support of what might be called the *religious* content of great poetry" and to Murry for the personal help he received in being published.[42] The same "religious" orientation of Murry has also been a source of disagreement with other critics, on such matters as the "regeneration" of Hamlet— opposed for example by E. M. W. Tillyard[43]—and the "last supper" interpretation of Antony's feast with Enobarbus, suggesting Judas—of which G. Wilson Knight approves[44] and Bonamy Dobrée disapproves.[45] (Murry's criticism here has echoes of D. H. Lawrence's "last supper," in which Murry was cast in the role of Judas.) Then there are certain subtle observations which have been generally accepted, such as Murry's comment on Shakespeare's brilliant use of "lass" rather than "queen" at the close of *Antony and Cleopatra*.[46]

In constructing the story of Shakespeare, Murry saves himself from an obvious fictional approach by using his own peculiar biographic mode. As with Keats, he is concerned with Shakespeare's "poetic life"; this interest keeps him in close contact with the work. For example, he attempts to recreate the "pupil" stage of Shakespeare's life, when the young poet and "theatre man" was learning from the scholar-wits, who notoriously resented his intrusion as a "play-tinkerer." Murry compares the devices which Shakespeare developed from patterns such as those used by Kyd and Marlowe. He takes a passage showing the "varied antiphonies" of Kyd's lines:

> Here lay my hope, and here my hope hath end:
> Here lay my heart, and here my heart was slain:
> Here lay my treasure, here my treasure lost:
> Here lay my bliss, and here my bliss bereft:
> But hope, heart, treasure, joy and bliss
> All fled, fail'd, died, yea all decay'd with this.

and compares it with the elaboration in a very early speech by the King in Shakespeare's *Henry VI, Part III* (only the beginning and end are given here):

> *King.* This battle fares like to the morning's war,
> When dying clouds contend with growing light,
> What time the shepherd, blowing of his nails,
> Can neither call it perfect day or night.
> Now sways it this way, like a mighty sea
> Forced by the tide to combat with the wind;
> Now sways it that way, like the self-same sea
> Forced to retire by fury of the wind:
> Sometime the flood prevails, and then the wind;
> Now one the better, then another best;
> Both tugging to be victors, breast to breast,
> Yet neither conqueror nor conquered:
> So in the equal poise of this fell war
> Here on this molehill will I sit me down.
> To who God will, there be the victory!
>   . . . . .
> And to conclude, the shepherd's homely curds,
> His cold thin drink out of his leather bottle,
> His wonted sleep under a fresh tree's shade,
> All which secure and sweetly he enjoys,
> Is far beyond a prince's delicates,
> His viands sparkling in a golden cup,

His body couched in a curious bed
When care, mistrust, and treason waits on him.[47]

What is developing in the passage just quoted and that which Shakespeare increasingly developed Murry calls lyricism: "that which springs from the first plenary sense of creative freedom and spontaneity, after a technique has been mastered." Lyricism, "a certain simple spontaneity," says Murry, "springs from the expansion of genius on a congenial theme"; it "is a first approach towards self-identification with a figure of the imagination"—towards "spontaneity," an all-important element in great poetry for Murry.[48] It is the key to the concept of "sensation" rather than "idea" as the true poetic experience, a notion which Murry took from Keats: "What Keats meant by 'sensation' was the spontaneous utterance of the total man through the imagination."[49]

As examples of poets who write "poetry of sensation" and "poetry of thought," Murry cites Shakespeare and Milton, respectively. Later in the book, in the chapter "Imagery and Imagination," Murry develops the "sensation" concept into "image-sensation" and "character-sensation." He gives as an example of the "image-sensation" that which developed from the apparent connection in Shakespeare's mind of fawning flattery with spaniels receiving sweetmeats from the nobility:[50] "the image, having its roots in some vital experience, grows steadily more complex; it takes on a life of its own until any part of it can suggest any other by no logical connection at all. The total image becomes, as it were, a living word for sickening flattery. It is what Keats would call the *sensation* of flattery, stored up in a self-renewing image."[51] He gives as example of the "character-sensation" several quotations from Cleopatra's speeches which give the sensation of Cleopatra at the time, the "lapsing consciousness," the "Death-Cleopatra-nurse-babe-Sleep" sensation as in

Where art thou, Death?
Come hither, come! come, come, and take a queen
Worth many babes and beggars.

· · · · ·

> Peace, peace!
> Dost thou not see my baby at my breast
> That sucks the nurse asleep?[52]

The phase of Shakespeare's life represented in the chapter "The Sonnet Story" is based upon Murry's apparent certainty that the famous "Mr. W. H." was Henry Wriothesley, or the Earl of Southampton. It was the story

of brief intoxication by a friendship with a young aristocrat; of quick disillusion; of a renewal of friendly relations on a quite different basis, when Shakespeare was economically independent; of a gradual decay of the relation, culminating years after in a breach of confidence which may have been mere carelessness on the patron's part, but if it were, was just as bitter to Shakespeare as any deliberate attempt to besmirch him would have been: perhaps more bitter, for it showed that he had been held in no esteem at all. He was not worth even the trouble of hating.[53]

The young aristocrat, Southampton, indecently handed over the sonnets to a printer—an act which probably accounted for the bitter play *Timon of Athens* of which one of the themes is patronage and ingratitude. Among the interesting reconsiderations that Murry's approach leads to, is that Sonnet 110 is not about Shakespeare's regretting his theatrical career but his introspectively accusing himself of having violated a true love by professing intimacy with new friends.[54] In this connection, Murry himself does not regret Shakespeare's involvement with drama; it did not spoil the poet—"quite the contrary. Drama is the highest and fullest form of poetry."[55]

After dealing as much as he can with the personal life of Shakespeare, Murry examines Shakespeare in relation to history and to England in particular. He centers his thoughts on the concern of *Heaven—and Earth:* the need for order. Shakespeare's view, Murry thinks, was near that of York's in *Richard II;* he is loyal to royalty insofar as it is the fount of order, as long as it stands as a manifestation of the divine principle of order. To York's attitude can be added the speech of Ulysses in *Troilus and Cressida* and the Shakespearean scene of *Sir Thomas More.* Superimposed on the basic history itself, Murry sees a "new imaginative succession," starting with the Bastard in *King John*—halfway through Shakespeare's historical work. Shakespeare's genius subordinates the historical: "Just as the Bastard by his being dwarfs the figures and events of history in *King John*, so Falstaff and Hotspur dwarf them in *Henry IV Part I*."[56]

Shakespeare's quest for the ideal Englishman, for so Murry regards it, who will bring order to the kingdom finishes with *Henry V*: "In *Henry V*, so to speak, the Bastard becomes the legitimate King of England."[57] Supporting his contention with quotations, Murry sees the Bastard as the "madcap" revolutionary Englishman with Harry Percy as his "lineal successor." Before, however, "his final avatar as Harry the King, the Bastard was to undergo an exciting metamorphosis. He was to divide by an imaginative fission, into Falstaff and Hotspur: into the cynical critic of honour, and its idolater. His bluntness and bravery into Harry Percy: his wit and humour into Jack Falstaff."[58] Their complementation can be seen particularly on the question of honor.

In the course of history, Hotspur was killed; and Shakespeare had to kill Falstaff. Prince Hal had to be brought back into history and this was done by something of a twist in his character—although his rejection of Falstaff can be read as more embarrassment than cruelty. Prince Hal had to do what he did for the sake of order:

> I am the Prince of Wales; and think not, Percy,
> To share with me in glory any more:
> Two stars keep not their motion in one sphere;
> Nor can one England brook a double reign.[59]

From now on—and after the death of Falstaff—Shakespeare is free to idealize Henry V, and to make him the true governor by both divine and natural right: *Henry V* is Shakespeare's "final answer to the question of divine right, and the problem of order. He passes beyond them both. That king is king indeed, who by his act and speech utters the soul of a people. He is king by right divine, and by right of nature: for these two rights are one."[60] Henry has made honor a reality; he is the imaginative embodiment of "organic and creative order."

We have returned to the main point of *Heaven—and Earth*,

the establishment of order—not just political order, though it is one facet—an imaginative order at the apex of which is the ideal Englishman. This is the apotheosis on the historical level; on the intellectual or spiritual level, there is what Murry calls "the Shakespeare Man" epitomized in Prince Hamlet: "Prince Hamlet *is* the Bastard, and Mercutio, and Benedick; he is that man, sprung from their root, debonair, gracious, generous, witty as they."[61] Murry develops this concept of "the Shakespeare Man," seeing, for example, the melancholy side of Hamlet enter into Antonio and Jaques:

> I hold the world but as the world, Gratiano;
> A stage where every man must play a part,
> And mine a sad one.
>   All the world's a stage,
> And all the men and women merely players:
> They have their exits and their entrances. . . .[62]

This melancholy develops in Hamlet to the great introspective question of "whether 'tis nobler," and on the answer to it Murry takes issue with Samuel Johnson. Johnson saw the choice in rational terms; for Murry, the question is one of contradiction which must be transcended, a Blakean dilemma of "the contraries without which there is no progression." Murry believes that Act V shows the transcendence in action, if not awareness, in Hamlet's "own final spontaneity."

Most of the other essays in *Shakespeare* apply Murry's critical criteria to specific plays and problems. Particularly good perhaps is the one on *Antony and Cleopatra* with the word "royal" as its operative center, and the variations and development of the royal natures of Antony and Cleopatra. In the essay on *The Merchant of Venice* he uses that play as an example of Shakespeare's method, essentially "the humanization of melodrama." This being so, Murry appeals to critics to recognize that the situation is a *donnée:* "His characters derive their first rudimentary life from the situation. Therefore, they are humanized rather than human"[63]—a concept which resembles Francis Fergusson's concept of Sophocles' characters as "actualization of the action."[64] Of *The Merchant of Venice* itself Murry observes that, more than any other of Shakespeare's plays, it is "a matter-of-fact fairy tale: a true folk story, made drama; and it makes its secular appeal to that primitive substance of the human consciousness whence folk-tales took their origin."[65] This conclusion is an interesting one to check with Freud's analysis of the plot as basic myth.[66]

The clue to an understanding of the three great tragedies—*Othello, Macbeth,* and *King Lear*—Murry sees in an awareness that Shakespeare accepted a melodramatic situation for his characters, and that there follows a discrepancy between character and act—as compared with the exception, *Hamlet,* in which the Prince has an inner development leading to catastrophe. In *Macbeth* in particular, Macbeth and Lady Macbeth perform their insane act, as it were, and then "suddenly emerge from their madness, and look upon their deed with the same naivety [*sic*] as we of the audience." The result is that in the very act of their diabolical murder, they "reveal themselves as naive and innocent." It is this sudden consciousness of the main action in the play, after their terrible deed, which "convulses our morality and awakens in us thoughts beyond the reaches of our souls."[67]

There is the same "terrible naivety [*sic*]" in Othello and Desdemona. In his criticism of *Othello* Murry begins with an explanation of the word "wonder" in Desdemona's line "Sure, there's some wonder in this handkerchief," and the reverberations—its importance as a love token, Othello's description of its magical origin, and the strangeness, in the opinion of Desdemona, of Othello's reactions. The article is a good answer to the famous footnote of T. S. Eliot that nobody had really answered Rymer's objections to *Othello,*[68] during the course of which Rymer satirically referred to the play as the *Tragedy of the Handkerchief.*

The essay on *King Lear,* as Murry admits in the preface to the later edition of *Shakespeare,* is strangely unsatisfactory. With the other plays Murry could, he felt, "penetrate to their imaginative centre." In *King Lear* he felt a basic contradiction, but, with the critical honesty typical of Murry, he acknowledges his lack of understanding. Finally, with *The Tempest,* Murry is more successful, partly because it suits his approach of seeing the play through the writer; and it is difficult to argue against the position that Prospero is "uniquely 'shot with' Shakespeare." To some extent, Murry regards *The Tempest* as an answer to Montaigne's favorable comparison of the savage as against the civilized. Shakespeare does not accept this comparison; man can improve on nature, though only through nature's art in man: "Nature and Nurture alone can make human Nature."[69] This goal is the conscious one of Prospero: "The Island is a realm where by Art or Nurture Prospero transforms man's Nature to true Human Nature."[70] But the transformation is not always possible: Caliban is one "on whose nature/Nurture can never stick; on whom my pains/Humanely taken, all, all lost, quite lost."

But Shakespeare's Prospero was visited at the end by a doubt: as he imagined, might he not be imagined? To what extent *was* it all a dream? And here Murry ends on a mystical note which can be, and has been, easily derided. At that moment, says Murry, Shakespeare "understood that Imagination was the world in which Innocence grew to ripeness, its blossom unshattered by Experience, his mind was turmoiled by the thought that Experience might be the Imagination of another Power.... Shakespeare's dream against God's; yet Shakespeare's dream is God's and Shakespeare God's dream. That is *The Tempest*."[71]

This kind of grandiose statement, taken out of context, has done much damage to Murry's reputation as a critic; but it should always be borne in mind that—to adapt what is almost a modern definition of God—Shakespeare is the "grounds of his being." In this attitude is Murry's weakness, causing flights into circular superlatives of admiration; but in it also lies the strength of his "high seriousness." His most earnest purpose was to reawaken Shakespeare as a cultural force in the average Englishman. To some extent he succeeded; it is notable that his three most successful books—*Shakespeare, Keats and Shakespeare,* and *The Problem of Style*—all deal to a greater or less extent with Shakespeare.

Not that he tried to "popularize" Shakespeare—a condescension of which he was not guilty. He would enter the lists with any scholar if he felt strongly enough—for example, against J. M. Robertson's attempt to show that between fifty and sixty of the sonnets usually attributed to Shakespeare were not written by him.[72] Shakespeare's work was constantly reexamined by Murry over the years, and he returned to essays to revise and correct them as new facts and new insights offered themselves. For this reason, it is better to look at the last version of his essays on Shakespeare (apart from those in the volume entitled *Shakespeare*), most of which he collected in his reissue of early essays in 1950.[73]

In these essays he uses the whole range of his critical gifts from general philosophical comments to close verbal analysis. "Shakespeare and Love" is a hymn of praise to Shakespeare as England's leading poet of love, with an application of the treatment of love in the plays to Shakespeare's own experience. Shakespeare, Murry feels, must have experienced a disastrous love affair, expressed at the time of the sonnets and "the Hamlet period," but he achieved a restored faith in the power of love as evidenced in the final plays such as *The Tempest*.[74]

In dealing with characters, Murry, like Charles Lamb, rejects any attempt to moralize about the creation of great comic character; Falstaff is an element in Shakespeare's rich fantasy. When Shakespeare, because of the pressure of the audience and royal command, tried to rehabilitate him, he only partially succeeded. John Falstaff of *Henry IV, Part I* never really lives in the esthetic imagination again.[75] At the other end of the scale in character types, Murry attempts to restore the greatness due to *Coriolanus* as a dramatic creation, seeing the play's protagonist as an example of the impulsive courageous "schoolboy" who must still prove himself to his mother. (As the First Citizen says, "Though soft-conscienced men can be content to say it was for his country, he did it to please his mother and to be partly proud.") Tied to this victim of the "Oedipus conflict" is that "neglected heroine," Virgilia, whom Coriolanus aptly calls "my gracious silence." Murry's sensitivity to the pregnant word or phrase is one of his most effective talents: Virgilia could be lost since she is given to us in only "two dozen words and a world of unspoken contrast." Murry restores her to us and makes, from his insights, some suggestions for textual emendation.[76]

Two of his essays depend almost entirely on his sense of a particular word. In "Shakespeare's Dedication" he shrewdly examines Shakespeare's first use of "dedication" in 1593, when it seems to be almost a synonym for self-surrender in love, and its degradation as a term associated with prostitution as used by Cressida, Macduff, and Iachimo. Murry must look for this change in the poet's experience, and finds it expressed by the poet at the beginning of *Timon of Athens*. In Murry's reconstruction, Shakespeare first used the word in dedicating his sonnets to the young Southampton, with whom he was infatuated; but he experienced a sudden revulsion of sentiment when the young lord handed over these intimate poems of affection for publication.[77]

In "The Mortal Moon" Murry takes the disputed passage in Sonnet 107—"The mortall Moone hath her eclipse indur'de"— and argues that this means (if the "mortall Moone" is the Queen, and not the crescent formation of the Spanish Armada, as one critic argued) not that "The Queen is dead" but "The Queen has recovered": for the normal meaning of "endure" in Shakespeare is "to suffer and survive." He follows through this meaning in the rest of the sonnet. Although it is for Shakespearean scholars to argue about these interpretations, Murry is always readable in his suggestions and evokes the atmosphere of exciting possibility even if one cannot always judge the rightness of his arguments.[78]

Some of his very best work on Shakespeare is in illustrative criticism, consisting of the examples he uses to demonstrate his arguments. In *The Problem of Style* he follows the structure of simile and metaphor through the death scene of Cleopatra. He examines the precise language which Shakespeare uses to express an infinite complexity; he reveals the subtle variations of a basic metaphor in "He tells her something/That makes her blood look out"; in "tonight I'll force/The wine peep through their scars"; and in other passages.[79] In "Metaphor," one of his most instructive essays, he uses examples to show "the self-creative progress" of Shakespeare's imagery; for instance, he examines closely the imagistic structure which Shakespeare built on the account of Cleopatra about Cydnus as given in North's *Plutarch,* and the means by which North's "inconsequential panorama" is given "an organic unity."[80] As one reads such examples one has to admire Murry's sensitive "taste"—much as Murry himself, like Wordsworth, distrusted the word.

That Murry was not always correct in some of his individual criticisms of Shakespeare's work made no difference to his fundamental attitude. Shakespeare was the fount of English culture—the great teacher-artist for Englishmen that Homer had been for the Greeks at one stage of history. If the language Murry uses about Shakespeare sounds "religious," as some critics have observed, it is because, in a sense, it *is*. Murry cannot avoid using the language of the trinity, for example, in explaining that Shakespeare "apprehended as realities a truth, a harmony, and a love—apprehended them as one and not as three"[81]—an apprehension, incidentally, which in Murry's view, reached its apex in "The Phoenix and the Turtle," a "symbolic vision of perfect and celestial love,"[82] and "the most perfect short poem in any language."[83]

It is notable that he also, in the superlatives he applies to this poem, says it is "platonic and mystical"[84]; it is, in fact, a perfect synthesis of the two strains in Murry, his platonic Hellenism and mystical Christianity. In the light of this synthesis, which Murry was always seeking, we must view his seemingly extravagant statements. Thus, he shrewdly comments on *Antony and Cleopatra* as a play of loyalty—Enobarbus, Eros, Antony, Cleopatra, Charmian, Iris, "one after another make the sacrifice" for the sake of fidelity. Yet there is a sense of serenity, "a profundity of calm." How can one account for this? Murry must turn to Christ for the answer: " 'Greater love hath no *man* than this that he lay down his life for a friend.' And Christ's own crucifixion is the archetype of all Shakespeare's tragedy."[85]

Giving a reason for speaking almost entirely on Shakespeare in the lecture announced as "The Nature of Poetry," Murry maintained that the title necessarily meant "the nature of Shakespeare's poetry."[86] Moreover, he observed in somewhat lighter vein: "I feel that if I had offered to lecture on Keats, or Reparations, or the Fascist movement, it would have turned out to be the same old thing. Shakespeare would have been the burden of my song."[87] For Murry, whatever he said would somehow have sprung from the supreme knowledge possessed by "William Shakespeare of Stratford-upon-Avon, Gentleman."

CHAPTER 6

The Meaning of Lawrence

ALTHOUGH Murry met D. H. Lawrence early in his career
—in his mid-twenties—and was closely associated with him for
only a few years, it took him a lifetime to try to absorb the fact
of Lawrence's genius. Almost the last act of Murry's life was to
put Lawrence into what he felt was a critical perspective; *Love,
Freedom and Society,* containing his most dispassionate study
of Lawrence and the one which, he told Frieda, he was sure was
his best, was published in 1957, the year of his death and
twenty-six years after his more celebrated *Son of Woman.* In
the many books and articles which appeared between these two
studies, Lawrence, next only to Keats and Shakespeare, was a
key figure, a basic force in life which Murry felt impelled to deal
with.

However, as a key figure, Lawrence was obviously in a different category from Keats and Shakespeare; he could not easily
be idealized because Murry had known him in the violent tu-
mult of existence and had quarreled with him bitterly. Lawrence was not a contemporary of the kind of T. S. Eliot, with
whom one could have a cerebral tussle and then leave things in
abeyance on an "agree to disagree" basis. To Lawrence, either
people had to be deeply and completely together in creation, or
they had to be apart, in destruction: "Let us live together and
create a new world ... here is all destruction and dying and
corruption, let us go away.... But let us go *together,* and keep
together, several of us, as being of one spirit. Let it be union in
the unconsciousness, not in the consciousness ... let us all try
to be happy *together,* in unanimity, not in hostility, creating, not
destroying."[1]

It is not surprising that Murry, who was to be part of this "union in the unconsciousness," found his position as critic almost

impossible. He could not stand critically apart from Lawrence; he was unable to use either his Classic sense of rational evaluation, or his more intimate and intuitive approach of discovering, and working from, the artist's "creative centre." Lawrence would not be "discovered." In his final letter to Murry he wrote: "We don't know one another—if you knew *how* little we know one another!"[2] But Murry had somehow to "know" the man in order to criticize his work. Murry never gave up the attempt, but his efforts have neither the settled and authoritative evaluative quality of his early essays nor the assured unity of a "poetic life."

Yet one cannot dismiss Murry's work as easily as most of the other memoirs of Lawrence. There have been—and are—a series of emotional whirlwinds circling around the fact of Lawrence, with little or no concern for literary values. To Murry's credit, he genuinely respected the superb genius of Lawrence and made an earnest effort, over his lifetime, to work away from a purely personal involvement to a more general conception of Lawrence. Murry's work enters the realm of literary criticism in the wide sense because he deals, not so much with the clash of two men as with that of two literary personalities—a creative genius and a critical talent. One may not want to term the resulting work "literary criticism" in a precise sense; *Lebensphilosophie*, or "life-wisdom," has been suggested, although this is somewhat begging the question since any worthy criticism is a form of life-wisdom. Still, the suggestion has a point. Where criticism (at least, Murry's form of evaluative criticism) suggests a construction on certain premises, *Lebensphilosophie* suggests a concern with the premises themselves, either the breaking of old ones or the establishing of new ones.

The spatial and constructional metaphor comes in well here. Murry was discussed in an earlier chapter as a "general critic," one concerned with restoring a living quality to the *topoi* of the race. He was—if one may be allowed to extend the term—a "topographer," and Lawrence felt he had found in Murry the man destined to be the "topographer" of his pioneering work. Murry would follow and map out the clearings pioneered by Lawrence and would articulate the structures to develop on the new premises. Lawrence spoke in almost exactly these terms when, soon after meeting Murry, he wrote enthusiastically of him: "he'll build up the temple if I carve out the way—the place."[3] This same idea motivated Lawrence's several attempts to persuade Murry to follow him to his visionary Rananim. For good reasons, Murry did not become the follower that Lawrence required; but he never ceased to worry about what he should have done.

The record of the association of Murry with Lawrence is important both as part of twentieth-century literary history and as the basis for understanding what Lawrence meant for Murry.

I *Son of Woman*

The two men first met in 1913 in Murry's office, which also served as a residence, in Chancery Lane, London. As a result of this meeting, Lawrence and Frieda, his wife-to-be, invited Murry and Katherine Mansfield to share holidays with them in England and Italy. On July 13 of the following year, Murry and Katherine were witnesses at the wedding of Lawrence and Frieda; and a few weeks later the two couples lived in nearby cottages in Buckinghamshire. It was not, Murry recalls in his autobiography, a happy time for any of them, particularly because of the effect of the war and Lawrence's quarrels with Frieda.[4] They found some solace in planning Lawrence's projected Utopia on an island to be called "Rananim." For Murry, life became very bleak when Katherine decided to leave him to go to France and when the Lawrences left for Greatham in Sussex. Murry followed the couple, and Lawrence looked after Murry when he was sick.

This period seems to have been the one of closest friendship between Lawrence and Murry, in which Lawrence even foresaw Murry's achievement being greater than his. Lawrence wrote to Lady Ottoline Morrell: "Murry is here because Katherine has gone to Paris. He is one of the men of the future—you will see. He is with me for the Revolution. He is just finishing his novel— his first—*very* good. At present he is my partner—the only man who quite simply is with me—One day he'll be ahead of me. Because he'll build up the temple if I carve out the way—the place."[5]

Katherine suddenly returned from Paris; and, during that summer of 1915, the two couples again lived near each other in

the Hampstead area of London. Lawrence and Murry cooper-
ated on a magazine called *The Signature,* which lasted for three
issues. Lawrence was bitter because of the suppression of *The
Rainbow,* and Katherine was deeply distressed by the death of
her brother in the war—so much so that, when she and Murry
went to France, he returned, resenting her excessive devotion to
the memory of her brother, and sought out Lawrence. However,
Lawrence wrote to Katherine that he was "not very much in
sympathy" with Murry and that he was sick of the "personal"
element: "It remains now whether Murry is still based upon the
personal hypothesis: because if he is, then our ways are different. I don't want a purely personal relation with him; he is a
man, therefore our relation should be based on *purpose;* not
upon that which we *are,* but upon that which we wish to bring
to pass." And he ended the letter: "We must grow from our
deepest underground roots, out of the *unconsciousness,* not from
the conscious concepts which we falsely call ourselves. Murry
irritates me and falsifies me, and I must tell him so. He makes
me false. If that must always be so, then there is no relation between us."[6]

But a week later Lawrence was writing that "There remain
only you and Murry in our lives. We look at the others as across
the grave." Murry himself returned to Katherine in the South
of France, where, during the first three months of 1916, they
spent the happiest period of their lives together. But Lawrence,
who seemed to need Murry at this time, wrote to them that he
felt they were his only friends in the world, and urged them to
join him and Frieda in Cornwall, even sketching for them detailed diagrams of a cottage he had found for them: "It would
be *so splendid ... such* a lovely place: our Rananim."[7] And he
was talking of a mystic blood-brotherhood: "No more quarrels
and quibbles. Let it be agreed for ever. I am *Blutbruder:* a
Blutbrüderschaft between us all."[8]

In spite of the fact that southern France suited Katherine,
they responded, not without misgivings, to Lawrence's urging.
There was soon disillusionment on the part of both men, and
the real break between them probably occurred at this time. As
Murry tells the story in Chapter xxvii of his autobiography, he
was bewildered by Lawrence's talk of "blood-brotherhood" and

by his hinting "at the need of some inviolable sacrament between us—some pre-Christian blood-rite in keeping with the primeval rocks about us."[9] As Murry drew back from such ideas, Lawrence became exasperated. Also, there were violent scenes between Frieda and Lawrence, and the tension became unbearable. One night, Murry records, "I heard him crying or moaning that I was 'an obscene bug that was sucking his life away,' and my blood went cold."[10] Murry and Katherine left for the south shore of Cornwall, and the two men saw little of each other after that.

The association continued but never again with the same intimacy. Lawrence's attitude to Murry was ambivalent; in the January following their separation, he wrote in a letter, "Murry fills me with loathing, still somehow I am fond of him."[11] As editor of *The Athenæum*, Murry invited Lawrence to contribute, accepting one contribution but rejecting another. Lawrence expressed his hostility by referring to Murry, in letters to friends, as the "small stinker," the "muckspout," and the "mudworm." But he made a considerable number of contributions to Murry's magazine *The Adelphi*, in which Murry began serializing *Fantasia of the Unconscious*. Lawrence's attacks on Christ helped to decrease the magazine's circulation by fifty per cent.

Lawrence made another attempt to persuade Murry to join him in a "new society," but Murry refused for good professional reasons. At a party which Lawrence gave in 1924 before he left for the new Rananim in America—the notorious "Last Supper" party—Lawrence is reported to have said to Murry, "Don't betray me," to which Murry replied: "I love you, Lorenzo, but I won't promise not to betray you." There have been several explanations of this mysterious statement, but Murry's version, as he gave it later, was: "I am full of affection for you and pity for what you are suffering; but I won't promise to conceal my knowledge of why you are suffering."[12] But H. T. Moore notes: "it is now known that Murry meant he would not betray Lawrence with Frieda, who had proposed that she and Murry become lovers."[13] The more specific explanation sounds reasonable in that Murry was in this year satirized in four of Lawrence's short stories. Nevertheless, the following year Lawrence invited Murry to Italy, but Murry had to refuse, mainly because of his wife's sickness; and with this refusal came the end of the relationship.

A few letters were exchanged in the last years of Lawrence's life but there is an increasing emphasis in Lawrence's letters on the "complete incompatibility" of the two that extends deeply into literature as well as personality: "I feel it's a betrayal of myself as a writer of what I mean, to go into the *Adelphi*, so I'd rather stay out."[14] In 1929, when Lawrence was ill in Mallorca, Murry offered to go to see him; and Lawrence replied in a noteworthy letter, kindly phrased ("felt so distressed about your wife," "my dear chap") but firm: "I know well that we 'missed it'.... We don't know one another—if you knew *how* little we know one another! .... Believe me, we belong to different worlds, different ways of consciousness, you and I, and the best we can do is to let one another alone, for ever and ever.... It is no good our meeting—even when we are immortal spirits, we shall dwell in different Hades. Why not accept it."[15] In 1930 Lawrence died, and in 1931 Murry's *Son of Woman: The Story of D. H. Lawrence* appeared.

Before *Son of Woman* Murry had written reviews of Lawrence's books, mainly in *The Athenæum* and *The Adelphi*, which were collected and published in *Reminiscences of D. H. Lawrence*.[16] The criticism in these reviews shows as much unevenness as the personal relationship of the two men. *Sons and Lovers* (1913) is hailed as "the most remarkable novel produced by any living Englishman under forty"—and "the achievement is not lessened by the author's subsequent decline." *The Lost Girl* (1920) and *Women in Love* (1920) demonstrate this "decay of Mr. D. H. Lawrence." In *Woman in Love* Murry sees no difference in the characters; they are all writhing in sex in an atmosphere of unintelligible phrases such as "suave loins of darkness" and "deep physical mind." For Murry it is all "bestial and sub-human," and he takes a stand for "consciousness" and "civilisation":

We stand by the consciousness and the civilisation of which the literature we know is the finest flower; Mr. Lawrence is in rebellion against both. If we try him before our court, he contemptuously rejects the jurisdiction. The things we prize are the things he would destroy; what is triumph to him is catastrophe to us. He is the outlaw of modern English literature; and he is the most interesting figure in it. But he must be shown no mercy.[17]

But in *Aaron's Rod* (1922) all is changed. Lawrence has become "a fountain of life" who far surpasses Joyce: "*Ulysses* is sterile; *Aaron's Rod* is full of the sap of life." Lawrence has gained "serenity," and his "philosophy" in the novel is as "vivid and vital" as the presentation of the characters. He comes near to attaining his theme, "the self-sufficiency of the human soul."

Similarly, Murry—showing considerable courage himself since Lawrence's remarks caused bitter opposition among his readership—approved of the *Fantasia of the Unconscious* (1922), giving credit to Lawrence for his courage in saying Christ had failed, particularly in respect to the problem of the man-woman relationship (although Murry reiterates his own belief in Christ as "the greatest human being of whom record remains"). *The Plumed Serpent* (1926), however, is disappointing—Lawrence may have "lost faith in his own imagination." In a review of *The Collected Poems* (1928), although the poetry is considered the work of genius, Lawrence is reproved for having no use for the "intellectual consciousness" at all: this is "well enough for him, with his sixth sense; but for the rest, who have only five, it is suicide." The remaining criticisms show the same divided approach: "D. H. Lawrence is a prophet and a great one, but he is not a wise man"; "He exalts the Body, because he is afraid to acknowledge the nature of the Soul"; "Mr. Lawrence has the tenderness; but he has *not* got the courage of it."

Murry, in fact, was off balance in these reviews in his criticism of Lawrence. Before he could steady himself and put Lawrence in critical perspective, he had to ask, and attempt to answer, a preliminary personal question. He does so in *Son of Woman;* and, because of this, it is a difficult book to classify. In a way, it is "pre-critical": one can argue against it, but not dismiss it. Mr. Mairet claims that, although it is a "strange" book, it remains "the most important book about Lawrence."[18] Certainly, it will always have the importance of, for example, the "early lives" of Milton; indeed, more than they, it breathes a sense of passionate involvement, of a living and sensitive association with the artist as man, that no later critic can recapture.

Perhaps Murry himself, in later years, was misleading about the true category of the book. He accepted the challenge of other critics and argued on critical grounds which were not his primary motivation at the time. The natural question for him was what had *happened* in his relationship with Lawrence. As he says in an introduction to a reissue of *Son of Woman,* the book was "primarily an effort to answer the question: why had we become antipodal to each other; why, as he put it in his final letter to me: 'Even when we are immortals spirits we shall dwell in different Hades.' "[19] Murry feels that somehow he had betrayed Lawrence—"the wrong I did to Lawrence was that I could not fulfil my duty as his friend."[20]

But there are different kinds of betrayal. Murry quite naturally became irritated with those followers of Lawrence who argued vehemently, but with little evidence, that he had betrayed Lawrence. On an ordinary "friendly" level, in fact, Murry showed considerable loyalty; he gave credit to Lawrence as a writer after Lawrence had made remarks about Katherine Mansfield which any husband would deeply resent, and, as the recently published edition of Frieda Lawrence's memoirs and correspondence reveal, he could be scrupulous in his respect for Lawrence: "I sometimes wonder [he says about the past] what would have happened if I had not had that awful feeling of loyalty in friendship to L."[21]

The "betrayal" of Lawrence was on a much deeper level, beyond the purely personal association. The nature of it was not obvious to Murry; it had to be sought out, and Murry applied his critical method to do so: he explored the man-artist in the work, although, since he was looking for the answer to a question, he treated the works of Lawrence, not formally as novel, story, and poem, but thematically as steps in a logical enquiry. Thus we have some unexpected verdicts on Lawrence's works. For example, since he wanted to explore at the deepest psychological level, it is not surprising that the essay *Fantasia of the Unconscious* should be Lawrence's greatest work.

The answer which Murry found to his basic question on the nature of his "betrayal," the conclusion of the book, is a strange one in that he decides he did not, in fact, tender the betrayal that Lawrence required: "This 'betrayal' was the one thing you lacked, the one thing I had to give, that you might shine forth among men as the thing of wonder that you were."[22] Murry argues that Lawrence fought against his own true destiny as a man who should have lived the life of the spirit. Lawrence refused to accept his calling; as a result, his problem was how "to overcome his own tenderness." Because, says Murry, his experience was such that he could not bear to accept his destiny, his great power for love became inverted into a power for hatred; the spiritual leader became a prophet of evil and negation. Lawrence was a Judas to his own truth; Murry's task as friend—and here he failed—was to be a Judas to this false side in Lawrence in order to correct the balance: "My duty as a friend to Lawrence was to be his pure enemy."[23]

The title, *Son of Woman,* indicates what Murry thinks caused Lawrence to deny his calling. From evidence in the novels and in other writings, such as *Fantasia of the Unconscious,* Murry shows, convincingly enough, that Lawrence's mother turned love which she could not give to her husband to Lawrence and overdevoted herself to him—an ill preparation for Lawrence's future association with women. Whether Murry should go on to say that this mother love made him incapable of wholeheartedly giving his love to another woman may be more doubtful; but, here again, he can quote Lawrence's own words in support.[24] His thesis is that Lawrence determined to escape his true destiny of spiritual awareness by transforming it into love of woman— of which he was not capable. Even sexually, Murry maintains, Lawrence was weak; certainly, he remained childless.

Having failed with woman, Lawrence wanted a perfect relationship with man—not on a physically homosexual level, but on a level of sex communion beyond the phallic, although still not purely spiritual. He sought a "sexuality of touch," a *Blutbrüderschaft* deeper than consciousness, in the mindless, premental sphere. This search also failed, so that Lawrence was thwarted in achieving the communion he wanted, or imagined he wanted, with both woman and man. When he determined to escape altogether the sterile intellectual consciousness of modern man, he tried to lose himself in admiration of a primitive and soulless people—which, says Murry, he also could not do.

Throughout *Son of Woman* Murry insists on the greatness of

Lawrence; there is, as Murry admits, truth in Huxley's famous remark that this book is a "piece of destructive hagiography." We must allow, however, that Murry recognized Lawrence's genius; and it should be borne in mind that he did, after all, have a special knowledge of Lawrence. On the level of the biography of a man, much of what Murry says would be difficult to confute, especially in the first part of the book. It would be resisting the obvious not to see Lawrence as Paul Morel in *Sons and Lovers,* trying unsuccessfully to break away from his mother, and as Cyril in *The White Peacock* (1911), retaining for his mother what he should have given "Miriam" and then "Clara Dawes." But, unfortunately, Murry's close personal experience of the details of Lawrence's life kept him close to the ground when he should have "taken wings" with the artist—or the prophet, or visionary, or "thought-adventurer." Whatever label we give to Lawrence, he was—to give another one—a "transformer" of experience. Murry tended to stay with the basic substance in which he was painfully involved.

It would not, however, be fair to leave the book as if it were purely a vehicle for Murry to prove something to himself. His critical talent, combined with his detailed knowledge of the text, opens the way for provocative insights. One may not want to go as far as Murry in seeing the "two Lawrences" in *The White Peacock*—"Cyril as the real Lawrence," "spiritual and feminine, the son of his mother"; and "Annable the man whom he dreamed that he might be," "physical and masculine."[25] But, at the same time, Murry's analysis clarifies the novel's thematic conflict.

This conflict, in fact, is a means of bringing the series of novels into unity. *The Rainbow* (1915) continues the story of "sexual failure." The Lawrence-hero yields to the woman; then he bitterly resents his dependence upon her. Lawrence tries to right this relationship of the male in *Women in Love*: "to make her subject again, to re-establish his own manhood—this is the secret purpose of *Women in Love.*" Along with this comes a new and related desire, "the hunger for a man," which in the novel is Rupert Birkin's desire for intimacy, semiphysical as well as semispiritual, with Gerald Crich (to some extent, an unfavorable portrait of Murry).[26]

For a brief period after Lawrence left England in 1919, there was, according to Murry, harmony between the conflicting elements in Lawrence; and it was during this period that Lawrence wrote what Murry calls his greatest book, *Fantasia of the Unconscious,* and his best novel, *Aaron's Rod.* For a critic to call *Fantasia of the Unconscious* his greatest book is a responsibility—as Murry is aware; but he argues that, although better "art" and "better shaped" books were produced by Lawrence's contemporaries, they were trivial beside the "major soul" of Lawrence revealed in these volumes. Lawrence "at bottom ... was not concerned with art"; and this lack of concern, Murry feels, is paradoxically proof of his eminence. Lawrence recognized that the conditions of great "art" are lacking in this era; "the artist today finds no spiritual authority which he instinctively acknowledges"—and art itself is not authority, only "the means by which authority may be revealed and expressed." Therefore, the great artist of today is concerned with discovering the authority "without which his activity as artist is either trivial or anarchic."

Murry asserts, in fact, that Lawrence "was neither a great novelist nor a great poet"; he was "the great life-adventurer of modern times," and *"Fantasia of the Unconscious* is his gospel."[27] It represents "a great and truly heroic effort to conquer his hatred, and to restore the spiritual man." More than this, Lawrence "consciously conceives it as his mission to create, or help to create, a world in which men so divided as himself shall be impossible."[28]

Fantasia of the Unconscious is given dramatic form in *Aaron's Rod.* But the novel is tragic because the Lawrence-hero cannot resolve the clash of spiritual detachment with the desire for human warmth, especially in the state of marriage: "From *Aaron's Rod*—the subtlest of all Lawrence's later books—we learn that he will never be able to maintain that supremacy of the spiritual over the physical, of the masculine-creative over the female-sexual, which he asserted in the *Fantasia."* And *Kangaroo* (1923) shows a continuation of this decline; "Somes-Lawrence" gives way—the woman becomes stronger: "Lawrence's fatal weakness is that his woman must believe in him, impersonally, or he cannot go forward. And the woman cannot believe in him, impersonally, while she knows that he depends upon her belief in him. It is impossible."[29]

Lawrence has to wait until he cooperates with Miss M. L. Skinner on a book, *The Boy in the Bush* (1924), to achieve a hero who is a "superman, the conqueror of woman and man and death alike."[30] The hero, Jack, "has conquered the division between the natural and the spiritual man, which has conquered Lawrence; conquered it, that is, as Lawrence dreamed it might be conquered." But Lawrence is not "Jack." In *The Plumed Serpent,* the self is given up, and he discards prophecy for "art" —perhaps his greatest work of "art," but much inferior to his great prophetic works. The work shows disintegration and a desire for revenge, but this phase is followed in turn by "a dream of resurrection" in such stories as "The Border Line" and "Glad Ghosts." (Incidentally, Murry is satirized in the latter story as "this cunning civilian, this subtle equivocator, this adjuster of the scales of truth.")

As Murry foresaw, critics accused him of ignoring Lawrence the artist. Aldous Huxley remarked that "the absurdity of [Mr. Murry's] critical method becomes the more manifest when we reflect that nobody would ever have heard of a Lawrence that was not an artist."[31] Some critics were not even sure that the book was about D. H. Lawrence. Graham Hough maintained that "the climax of methodological absurdity is reached by Middleton Murry, who begins his *Son of Woman* by saying that 'there can be but one true life of Lawrence; and it is contained in his works'; and then proceeds throughout to blame the works for not telling the story right."[32] F. R. Leavis in *Scrutiny*, went one step further: it was just "another book about Mr. Middleton Murry."[33] Murry, Leavis said, used Lawrence's works as "documentation" to define Lawrence as man, even as a psychological case history, rather than as artist and as genius.

In addition to Murry's attempt to forestall this objection when he first wrote *Son of Woman,* Murry defended his approach in his introduction to a new edition of *Son of Woman* in 1954; and in *Love, Freedom and Society,* published in 1957, he did not give ground. Leavis replied in *Scrutiny* to Murry's declaration that Lawrence was not primarily an artist, and made use of a quotation from Lawrence: "It is true that the Art of Flaubert was not his aim, but it is not for nothing that he writes, 'Art speech is the only speech.' "[34] But Murry could also quote Lawrence in retorting to this attitude:

to concentrate on his literary genius, and to ignore to what purpose he employed it is a kind of outrage to his spirit. Certainly it is a defiance of his own warnings. "Not the work I shall produce, but the real Me I shall achieve: that is the consideration," he had written in the critical winter of 1914-15. And we cannot, except by violence, avoid that consideration. The process of the gradual achievement of "the real Me"—the conquests and defeats of that struggle—are enmeshed in the intimate substance of his work.[35]

Murry's argument cannot be easily dismissed, but it might have had more force if he could have allowed himself a more imaginative concept of "the real Me" as applied to Lawrence—a "Me" which included the wholeness of the artist and his "art." As it was, he applied the standards of Realism too earnestly in his attempt to understand the "life-adventure" of Lawrence. The debate over Lawrence's novella *St. Mawr* (1925) is a good illustration of the weakness in Murry's approach.

Murry's first reaction to this story in his original review was that it "is a story which grows"; but he did not let it grow on him. He tried to place it in the general theoretical framework of *Son of Woman,* but it was one of Lawrence's works which fitted least: " 'Why can't men get their life straight like St. Mawr, and then think?' asks Lou. It seems [says Murry] a sound question, and is a foolish one; as though thinking were not life, and in equal need of straightening." There is a captious note in Murry's summary of the plot: "What Lou needs is the human equivalent of St. Mawr; a sterile stallion. But these are as scarce in the human world as in the animal. In other words, she is, like Teresa [in *The Plumed Serpent*], one of the new women whom Lawrence imagines for himself, and since she talks more, she is more tiresome and less real even than Teresa."

Murry goes on to comment that, "since the central conception is incoherent, the story itself is futile"; it is a "tissue of dishonesties"—"one long and unworthy evasion"—"a monument of Lawrence's disintegration."[36] If Murry had followed his original intuition and had let the story "grow" on him (as he did earlier with his best criticism), it would have achieved its own integration. For it is a story which "grows on you," partly because it touches a mythic level—one recalls how much the beauty and the strength of the horse have appealed to the literary mind of man, with Pegasus, the Houyhnhnms, Roan Stallion, and so on —and partly because, as Leavis points out, it is beautifully orchestrated. For instance—as if in answer to Murry's objection— Leavis shows how Lawrence illustrates his general point of getting "life straight" before beginning to "think": St. Mawr represents "life-impulsion, he stands for the sure intuition, the warning perception, of the vitally dangerous, the wrong path; he stands for the warning intuition of evil and disaster. He rightly balks at the adder; but his rider—assertively developed, insulated head and 'speaking' face—blindly and brutally ignores the living sentience beneath him."[37]

The debate over *St. Mawr* is also interesting because it brings into the picture T. S. Eliot, the adversary-friend of Murry. The theme of *St. Mawr* is similar to that of *The Cocktail Party* in that a young woman, dissatisfied with human male love, leaves her society to find a higher, more mysterious love. Leavis rates Lawrence's short story well above Eliot's work, and Murry adopts a formal tone in replying to him: "To contend, as Dr. Leavis does in his book, *D. H. Lawrence: Novelist,* that it [*St. Mawr*] is, in itself, immeasurably superior to *The Cocktail Party,* because of its greater spiritual depth and its absence of snobbery, is a kind of critical perversity.... As a work of art, *The Cocktail Party* has it."[38]

The debate over *St. Mawr* brings out a fundamental difference between Lawrence and Murry. Even though we allow Murry his point that Lawrence was greater as a prophet than as an artist, Murry himself was not, like Lawrence, a visionary who traveled restlessly until his death, or who attempted to live in the vision. He was, as has been previously suggested, more of the reformer whose existence was on a plane between mystical glimpses of the "new dispensation" and the desire for normalcy and even tradition. The nature of this difference between the two men is indicated by Murry's unfavorable view of *St. Mawr* as compared with his favorable view of Benjamin Constant's novella, *Adolphe*.

Murry published, together with a translation of *Adolphe,* a long critical essay, "The Conquest of Death."[39] He heartily approves of Constant's story. In plot, it is similar to *St. Mawr* in that both stories involve heroines capable of strong and devoted love; but they are caught in a setting of sophisticated decadence, a particularly male decadence in which man has lost his instinctive power and is weakened by a divided consciousness. But the resolutions are different: in *St. Mawr* the heroine leaves the contemporary male world and wishes, she says, "with all my soul, that some men *were* bigger and stronger and *deeper* than I am." In *Adolphe*—or in the interpretation which Murry gives to it— the heroine dies because the man cannot achieve the same all-giving love and loyalty of which she is capable. If he could have loved her as she loved him, all, presumably, would have been well.

Lawrence at the end of his story and Murry at the end of his criticism make comments which reveal the distance between the uncompromising visionary and the liberal-minded conservative. At the end of *St. Mawr* the heroine is imbued with a spirit that is "bigger than men, bigger than people, bigger than religion"; in his commentary on *Adolphe* Murry ends with a plea that, in a spirit of "liberalism," we accept—with "imaginative reservations"—the "humane necessity of the traditional forms of the Christian religion."

II *Lawrence as a Life Force*

In his constant reference to Lawrence after *Son of Woman,* Murry does not deny the theme of that book so much as he changes the tone from one of personal and psychological self-involvement to one of religious and social significance. He had attempted to express his philosophical difference from Lawrence in *God: An Introduction to the Science of Metabiology,* published two years before *Son of Woman.* He agreed with Lawrence on the necessity for a spiritual regeneration "passing beyond the intellectual consciousness."[40] But, as in *Son of Woman,* he feels that Lawrence betrayed his basic insight: really of the same nature as Christ, Lawrence repudiated Christian "love." Because he was afraid to acknowledge the truth of the "metabiological" (as opposed to the "biological"—the two terms are roughly an aspect of the body-soul debate), he overempha-

sizes the "body" and dreams of a return to a preintellectual primitive and instinctive state. But we cannot return to such "na-
turalism." Perhaps life in the Western world has taken the
wrong turn, but, says Murry, instead of rejecting our "intellectual heritage," we should push forward beyond it. Murry accepts
Lawrence as a great prophet, but "he is not a wise man"; and
modern prophets must be wise.[41]

* Throughout the 1930's and 1940's Murry never ceased to
worry about the significance of Lawrence. His intuition told
him that here was the great contemporary thought-adventurer—
but he could not agree with him. He compares him with other
vatic poets. In *William Blake* (1933) Lawrence has similarities
with Blake; they both envision a "perfection of human existence
continually glimpsed and intermittently experienced," although
Blake places such a Golden Age in "the Eternity which preceded
the Fall," and Lawrence, "with his more modern historical habit,
places it among the old Etruscans."[42]

They both had a period when they questioned the truth of
Christ because He had flinched "from the true experience of
sex";[43] but the difference is in Lawrence's overemphasis of the
body. Both Blake and Lawrence, says Murry, "preached with
impassioned sincerity a doctrine of sexual regeneration: of regeneration of sex, and regeneration through sex." But "in
Blake the doctrine flows out of a larger doctrine from the beginning: all that is implicit in the experience and the conviction of
the living unity of the Body and the Soul. Therefore Blake was
proof against the error, into which Lawrence not seldom fell, of
asserting the Body and denying the Soul. And when he does this
Lawrence drives division deeper; in Blake the division is transcended from the beginning. For all their startling resemblances,
the doctrine of Blake belongs to a higher order."[44]

In 1944 Murry published *Adam and Eve: An Essay Towards
a New and Better Society,* and it contains a chapter entitled
"The Significance of D. H. Lawrence,"[45] which begins "Where
was Lawrence wrong?" Murry is very definite at this stage. Lawrence was right in preaching "individual sex-fulfilment as the
necessary basis of a regenerated society," but he was wrong in
preaching "that this individual sex-fulfilment must be sought
and achieved in permanent rebellion against the Christian doc-

trine of love." Lawrence was right in trying to revive a sense of mysterious authority based, not on a celibate, or mentally celibate, priesthood, but on a fully creative man-woman relationship; that is, "the father was to be the priest as well." Lawrence was wrong, however, in trying to replace the "God-authority." Lawrence felt he had to reject Christianity in order to bridge the gap from early asceticism and to give obedience to the more instinctual "dark gods." Murry felt that the regenerated sex relationship was a truer state of Christ. Incidentally, Murry contrasts Lawrence with Aldous Huxley, who, says Murry, used Lawrence as sanction for his own "nihilistic antinomianism": "But no two attitudes could be more antithetical than Lawrence's antinomianism and Huxley's—Huxley's bent on devaluing all human experience to a universal indifference, Lawrence's bent on giving significance to all human experience at whatever cost."

But no matter how definite Murry seemed to be at this time in interpreting Lawrence for himself, he was still pondering over him; and thirteen years after *Adam and Eve,* in the year of Murry's death, he published what he felt was his most important essay on Lawrence, in *Love, Freedom and Society.* Murry compares him, not with a literary person, but with another pioneer in the search for a new spiritual basis in life, Albert Schweitzer. The two were similar in that they both looked to forms of love to save society, and both turned away from modern mechanized civilization to primitive social groups. In his final summing up, Murry gives his own views. While acknowledging the greatness of these two prophets, Murry feels that, in the solutions they offer, although they are antipodal, each has a basic flaw; however, the opposition can be transcended in a superior synthesis. Although not directly critical in relation to literature, his final section, "Beyond the Prophets," is the culmination of "soul-making" applied to society—the development of a social contract in which the values and ideas of the great literary artists become the principles and acts of existence. In a combined literal and religious sense, the Christian story is the supreme and ennobling tragedy.

Much of the first essay on Lawrence (each of the three sections of *Love, Freedom and Society* contains two essays) deals with the discussion on *St. Mawr* and the comparison with *The Cocktail Party,* and Murry's answer to Leavis.[46] Murry continues to insist that, in any appraisal, there must be a consideration of the "total Lawrence," including his "daimon," and not merely of a particular "artistic" Lawrence. In fact, Lawrence was primarily important because he was "the most significant man of religion of the modern age." His destiny was to act on Blake's dictum, "All that can be annihilated, must be annihilated"; he was "the man of genius on whom fell the command to annihilate all that was annihilable in the bogus religion of his time, which is ours."[47]

On the more constructive side of life, however, Lawrence is "radically incoherent." On one hand, he asserts that industrial democracy is a lie because men are incapable of genuine love for each other; but, on the other, his work reveals repeatedly a concern and even affection for his fellowmen. He is anti-machine, although, with a little thought, Lawrence must have realized that the machine has ended much human slavery. Insofar as he refused to allow automatism to corrupt the human mind, Murry wholeheartedly agrees with him; in fact, he regards him as the "counter-prophet" of Karl Marx: "Lawrence envisions a millennium but only through the abolition of the machine; Marx envisions a millennium created by the machine."

Murry was extremely anti-Communist at this stage—even supporting a defensive war against Russia—and digresses somewhat into a tirade against Communism, which he views as a religion directly opposed to "the religion implicit in democracy." Lawrence could not admit faith in this "Christian civilization"; he felt it had to die and be replaced—as he maintains in his *Last Poems* (1932) and "The Man Who Died" (1929)—by a new consciousness based on physical tenderness and a truer man-woman relationship. However, according to Murry, the main reward for studying Lawrence is not a rational conclusion, but an annihilation of the false, and the resulting purification: "By discovering what Lawrence was, we discover what we are."[48]

Lawrence's approach is irrational, completely opposite to that of Schweitzer, with whom Murry deals in the next essay. Murry is not, one feels, as much at home with Schweitzer as with Lawrence.[49] However, what is more important for Murry than the arguments involved is Schweitzer's conviction that altruistic effort results from rational analysis, that ethics is a necessity of thought. In the final paragraph of this section on Schweitzer, there is a summing-up of the difference in the outlook of Lawrence and Schweitzer, at least the difference that concerns Murry:

I think I understand, at least in part, Schweitzer's motive, in so far as it came from the bleak and desperate feeling, akin to Lawrence's, that Christian civilisation had proved itself a mockery in the First World War; and that, unless there were some revolutionary renewal of love from some primal, untapped, virgin source, it was doomed. Lawrence sought this in the pristine instincts, Schweitzer in elemental thought. The purpose of both was to make a new reality of love. Both were driven to re-imagine the Kingdom of God. And both were compelled to set an abyss between it and the disheartening present. They are antipodal to one another. Schweitzer put all his confidence in rational thinking; Lawrence all his in our blood and bodies. "My great religion is a belief in the blood, the flesh, as being wiser than the intellect. We can go wrong in our minds. But what our blood feels and believes and says is always true." Schweitzer went wrong in his mind, Lawrence went wrong in his blood. And both went wrong for the same reason. They forgot that love was there at the beginning: it was the cause of their despair.[50]

Both men went wrong, and from the calmer distance Murry tries to evaluate the two sides and put their attitudes in perspective in the section "Beyond the Prophets." In the first essay, "Religion and the Free Society,"[51] much as he admires them, he virtually accuses them of *le trahison des clercs*. They "turn away from the humdrum and precious society to which they owe their own freedom to be themselves." They fail to see that however imperfect modern society is—and, Murry notes, they both forget "how recent in the perspective of history the industrial and humanitarian society really is"—it has sprung from the love ethic of Christ, of which the Cross is the central symbol. Murry finds that the attitudes of Schweitzer and Lawrence to the Cross are of special significance in that Schweitzer regards it as only a noble sentiment, of little importance in relation to the "ethic of altruism," while Lawrence rejects it as a "ghastly mistake." Lawrence agrees with Dostoevsky's Grand Inquisitor that Christ expected too much of man, whereas the Inquisitor was kinder in that he took men as they are.

In "The Man Who Died"—which "ranks with *The Grand Inquisitor* as a truly profound utterance of this age of the dissolution of the Christian consciousness"—Lawrence represents a risen Christ as repudiating his own gospel, as "resigning himself to the unconquerable distinction between the slavish and noble natures among men, and finding wholeness again in the bodily and sacramental love between himself and the priestess of Isis." Murry refuses to accept such exclusive aristocracy. The "free society" of modern democratic England has love as its nexus, even though it is "a commonplace sort of love, no doubt." Murry then develops his own point of view in the last essay, "Christianity and Tragedy."[52]

Unfortunately, the word "commonplace" has unpleasant associations nowadays, denoting the cheap and the vulgar. If the term could be understood more in the context of the best that is attainable for the ordinary man, it might well be applied to Murry, distinguishing him from the visionary world in which Lawrence lived. He could not follow Lawrence to Rananim, and Lawrence considered this a Satanic revolt: Murry, he wrote, after they had virtually parted ways in 1916, was "utterly unwilling to take himself for what he is, a clever, but non-original, non-creative individual. . . . I dislike him that he must assume himself the equal of the highest. That is the very essence of his malady, and all his twist and struggle is to make this falsehood appear a truth to himself."[53]

Murry's was not, however, the revolt of Satan but of Judas. Murry knew himself a hero worshipper, not a hero; and he wanted to "betray" his hero away from Rananim back to ordinary society, where he would be a great social leader. The ideal must somehow be brought into the ordinary, even if the result was only a "commonplace sort of love." His work on Lawrence was an attempt to incorporate the life and art of Lawrence as a force in the Christian humanist tradition. If it was not exactly literary, it was cultural criticism, the reassessment of premises to serve as a foundation for a more direct evaluation of life and literature.

CHAPTER 7

Unprofessional Essays

SIX months before he died, Murry wrote in his journal: "I have the feeling that I have been completely outside the main stream of literature: that I don't 'belong' and indeed never have belonged. My concern has always been that of a moralist, and I have never been sufficient of the artist to be diverted from it. And yet the stubborn feeling persists that my 'concern' was shared in the old days by Lawrence and by Katherine: that I was, in some sense, their critical counterpart, and that the *kind* of seriousness we had has been lost. That distinguished us, absolutely, from the Bloomsburies. Eliot came nearer to it; but from him, too, there was an inevitable separation. None of us was, or ever could have become, capable of accepting dogmatic Christianity, as Eliot did. I am the sole remaining representative of our particular integrity, our particular concern. We were all socially outsiders, quite without the social and domestic tradition which the Bloomsburies, Aldous Huxley, and expatriate— *plus royaliste que le roi*—Eliot inherited. And, I think, experience came more naked and direct to us than to the others. To us, there was a sense in which they were all 'phoneys' (in the nuance of [Salinger's] *The Catcher in the Rye*). Love meant more to us: we needed it more."[1]

A few years before he had made a similar entry: "To this search for integrity—the reconciliation of Heart and Mind, Emotion and Intellect—I have sacrificed whatever talent for art I possessed. It was, probably, not much: but I think I had the makings of a good literary critic. But it was not really, or not wholly, a sacrifice: for criticism (as I wanted to practise it anyhow) depended on values—a determination of what is good for man: τὸ εὖ ζῆν. And I had to find out."[2]

Along with the sense of acceptance of destiny, there is perhaps a note of regret in the remark "but I think I had the makings of a good literary critic." It recalls the advice which Lawrence gave him, that he "must stick to criticism," and it invites speculation on what his total contribution would have been if he had "stuck to his last" and had intellectually developed some of his original insights—if he had perhaps, after his rich experience of the 1920's, accepted a university position and dedicated himself in the manner of "Walter Pater or somebody of that style" (as Lawrence said). Certainly, two of his best books, *The Problem of Style* and *William Blake,* were produced under academic sponsorship.

Such speculation as regards Murry himself is no doubt idle, for he had the strong Romantic urge for personal experience, the need to find out for himself; and such experience, he felt, was almost the opposite to the academic life. He made the point on several occasions; for example, in a review entitled "Professors and Poets," he commented on the "professional" professor who does not, like the poet, "meet life naked." The poet "takes risks, he adventures himself"; but professors tend "to resent the 'life-adventure.' "[3] His objection, he felt, was confirmed by the fashion in which academic criticism had developed. In the journal of his last years, he deplores the "vast web of super-subtlety" of recent criticism; somehow the "life-giving, life-changing contact between the reader and the book"[4] had oozed out.

In one of the last reviews he wrote—perhaps the last one—he examined books of essays by R. P. Blackmur and Allen Tate; and he used this opportunity to protest against "the academic pressure working to make the study of English literature an intellectual discipline as rigorous as the study of the old classical humanities, or the new natural sciences." He takes exception to what at that time was being called "the new criticism"—"its complexity, its intensity, its scholasticism, its concentration on a narrow range of subject-matter—'the set subjects of our civilisation.' "[5]

Although Murry does not appear to appreciate the more positive qualities of new critical methods, the general questions he raises by his life and writing are relevant and important to contemporary criticism: can we lose the gift of "experience," difficult as it is to define? Do we suffer in the appreciation of art without it? Is professionalism depriving man of the finer elements of the amateur quality—elements of love, carefree response, immediacy and generosity in giving? These are old questions, but to pose them was part of Murry's contribution to criticism: to put life into the old questions.

The path that Murry chose after the mid-1920's took him increasingly away from specifically literary criticism into the realms of religion and politics. He used literature in an attempt to understand the totality and conduct of life. The high point of this approach in his writing was *Heaven—and Earth* (1938), in which he sought to explain the history of Western Christian humanism in a cycle from Chaucer to William Morris, and to find a direction for the future.[6] Never afraid to challenge the largest issues of man, he wrote books on Christ and God and applied himself to the problems of love and freedom in society in such books as *Adam and Eve* and *The Free Society*.

At the same time, Murry's need to demonstrate that he was "at bottom a good sound literary critic"[7] asserted itself, especially in later years, in such works as *Jonathan Swift* and *Unprofessional Essays*—so titled because, for the first time, he could engage in literary criticism without thinking of financial income. During no period did Murry altogether relinquish literary criticism—to do so would have been impossible in any circumstances because he could not separate his interests in this way: thus, when he was offered a fellowship by Liverpool University in the early 1930's, he studied William Blake intensely for two years, producing a book on him in the year following the publication of one called *The Necessity of Communism*.

I   *Blake and Christian Community*

Although Murry applied as best he could his considerable critical gifts to *William Blake,* most critics at this period agreed with the one in *Scrutiny* who lamented: "one cannot help feeling that for Mr. Murry to desert criticism of this type [as in *The Problem of Style*] for windy pseudo-religious 'interpretation' is a great loss to literature."[8] Murry, of course, would never have agreed that he was guilty of such desertion. Certainly, even if he could be said to have deserted "criticism," he never deserted the literary text. This fact is sometimes overlooked by those who object to his method. It is gratifying to know that the balance is being redressed; for example, a recent *Blake Bibliography* gives a very reasonable summary from a modern academic point of view:

A much more reliable work [than the one just discussed], also based almost wholly on Blake's text, is J. Middleton Murry's *William Blake* (1933). Some critics have ignored this book because it reflects Murry's current interest in a kind of Christian Marxism, but it should not be so easily dismissed. Murry's is not a study that often gets down to minute particulars, for he was primarily interested in ideas. But in his interpretation of Blake's ideas he remained largely faithful to the text, and his study is extremely helpful in understanding important matters like the contraries. Since an extra-Blakean thesis does lurk beneath much of what is said, however, this book is idiosyncratic enough to require some sophistication of the reader.[9]

William Blake is an unusual book, and perhaps the best way to understand it is to start with the "extra-Blakean." It is helpful to see it in relation not only to Murry's own domestic troubles at the time[10] but also to the other books he wrote during the late 1920's and 1930's. *William Blake* is sandwiched in between the religious and political writings which form Murry's system or doctrine of thought; and this context causes some difficulty in Murry's critical diction. Murry could more easily transfer terms from one subject to another than most of his readers because he had little sense of "separateness"; thus, as well as being a pacifist, Blake was "A great Communist."[11] This category would not seem out of place to the Murry who, a few years later in *The Necessity of Pacifism*, was writing: "The dynamic of Socialism must be sought in the ideal of human brotherhood, in which today economic necessity and the spiritual imperative converge."[12] Blake was part of his total view of Christian living, and a similar terminology could be used throughout.

But there was a more serious dilemma, one which Murry never completely resolved: on the one hand, he tried to be the "Keatsian" critic who, without prejudice or preconceived ideas, opened himself receptively to Blake and worked from his "creative centre"; on the other hand, he was "very deliberately" restricting himself to "Blake's doctrine."[13]   Moreover, it would be most surprising if this doctrine did not have a number of points in common with the doctrine that Murry was developing for himself at this time.   There is, for example, in Murry's interpretation of Blake's thought an evolutionary quality which was natural to Murry and on which he built his *God: An Introduction to the Science of Metabiology,* with its dualist evolutionism on the levels of biology and "metabiology."   It is, however, particularly difficult to incorporate a *lyrical* poet into an evolutionary ideology; it is easy to underemphasize or ignore the lyrical quality.   It may be for this reason that Murry's friend, Max Plowman, also a Blake expert—although very much approving of the book and of Murry's critical approach of "imaginative re-entry into experience"—complained that Murry missed the "joy" in Blake.   Blake knew that "joy" is man's spiritual goal, says Plowman; but Murry could not appreciate this: "The joy in Blake fascinates him, but it is foreign to his thought."[14]

To attempt to relate a poet's work to the experience of the poet as man is also more difficult with a lyrical visionary such as Blake than with lyrical dramatists such as Shakespeare and even Keats.   Nevertheless, Murry undertakes this task.   He believes that Blake had to resolve two great problems in his life, the domestic one with his wife[15] and the political or historical one, with particular reference to the French Revolution; Blake wished to see his personal and human experience *sub specie æternitatis:* "This inextricable mingling of personal and impersonal, of Time with Eternity, belongs to the inmost of Blake's imaginative method.   His unremitting effort was to see his own life as the revelation of Eternity."[16]

With this understanding of Blake's purpose, Murry begins his close textual analysis; but to follow the many examples and allusions of Murry would require a long study in itself.   Among the many rewards of following Murry through the Prophetic Books is that—whether one agrees with his intentions or not—one sees new "wholes" in Blake's work; for example, Murry develops the Milton theme from *The Marriage of Heaven and Hell* in which Milton's Satan was the Messiah and Milton's God the Father was the Devil: "Thus Heaven and Hell were transposed and married.   Since then Blake had learned, at a price, that the Heaven and Hell he had so blithely married were both alike Hell. Not only was Milton's Jehovah-God Satan, but Milton's Satan was Satan, too; and they were both one, the Selfhood, the State of War."[17] Milton's imaginative regeneration was, Murry continues, the theme of Blake's *Milton,* his "prophetic masterpiece."[18] As Blake ceaselessly emphasized, selfhood must be continually annihilated. Murry guides the reader through the difficult symbolism until Milton is restored to Eternity, which is Forgiveness. Milton has learned to forgive: "It is Blake's teaching of this final unity between Eternity and Forgiveness which makes him great among the greatest."[19]

Later, in a review of Denis Saurat's book *Blake and Milton,* Murry takes the author to task for not dealing with this development in Blake of Milton's visionary redemption. It is not enough to see Milton as reason and Blake as energy in *The Marriage of Heaven and Hell,* in which the traditional "reason-over-energy" becomes the romantic "energy-over-reason." Blake goes further. In the next stage Reason and Energy fight, symbolized in the struggle of Urizen and Luvah-Orc to annihilate each other, and this "internecine struggle" is the real Satan. This Satan too must be defeated, and this is done in the regeneration of Milton: "What Milton could not achieve in his actual life, he achieves in the new existence which he enters in Blake's imagination—he learns the secret of Forgiveness." Blake ultimately transcends Satan with forgiveness, and gives Milton a new consciousness.[20]

"The new existence" and "the new consciousness" from Blake, or "the new dispensation" from Dostoevsky, or the "new great wave of love" from Lawrence—this is what Murry expected from genius. The greatest example of such genius—although a human, not a supernatural genius, Murry is careful to explain—was Christ. In order to make Christ "wholly *real*" to himself, in 1926 Murry wrote *The Life of Jesus* (the American title is *Jesus, Man of Genius*), which was followed three years later by *God: An Introduction to the Science of Metabiology.* The last book was an attempt to bring together Murry's experiences in life and literature and especially to point up a way of life based on the overwhelming mystical experience which followed Katherine Mansfield's death, although not through mystical disciplines

(which he soon gave up) but through conscious human understanding. He found in Christ the basic pattern for his purpose.
Christ too began with a mystical intuition, in His belief that
He had found the true God. He was the "new man" and He was
obedient to His "newness." He evolved with "organic coher-
ence" but on "a higher level than the pure biological."[21] This
higher—although still human—evolution Murry terms "metabiological."

Unlike *William Blake* and *God, The Life of Jesus* was a popular book; but the reasons for the popularity are suspect. Murry
makes the life of Christ sound frequently like a semifictional
news story, and he uses some of the rhetorical tricks he deplored
in *The Problem of Style*. There are melodramatic dialogues,
rhetorical questions, word repetition, and the building up of
vague emotive statement. An example is the scene on the lake:

> "Master!" they cried. "Don't you care whether we all are drowned?"
> "Why are you such cowards?" he said. "How can it be you have no
> faith?"
> He had no need to tell the waves to be silent. He had faith and
> was unafraid; he knew that it was not God's will that he should die
> before his destiny was accomplished. And when his men looked upon
> his perfect serenity, the fear began to leave their hearts. The storm
> became less terrible, and they rowed on into calm.
> Such, or like this, was the "miracle"; and it was a miracle, the only
> sort of miracle that has meaning for grown men—the miracle whereby
> a hero creates heroes. At the breath of the pure spirit the embers of
> men's souls become a flame.[22]

Murry's method of psychological identification with his subject
and of interpretation from the "creative centre" shows itself in a
way which, if it were typical, would justify those who are hostile
to this method. For example, some of the thought processes in
Christ's mind are unconvincingly facile, to say the least:

> "Are *you* He that should come, or must we wait for another?"
> With that question the little seed of a great certainty was sown in
> Jesus' heart. Might he not, after all, be the One?
> Yet how could he be the One? He was no son of David's line; his
> had been no triumphant epiphany; he was simply a teacher and a

prophet. Nay more, he was outcast and fugitive, hiding in the mountains—"a man of sorrows and acquainted with grief."
The wonderful vision of Isaiah flooded his mind.[23]

In the 1930's his books on non-literary—or comparatively non-literary—subjects appear, at first sight, to be more political than religious, but the change was a development rather than a new approach. In *The Necessity of Communism* (1932) and in *The Defence of Democracy* (1939), for example, there is a development of Murry's concern with the Christian principle of living. In *The Defence of Democracy* he makes such remarks as "The classless society is ... inconceivable except as a Christian society" and "A Christianity that includes Marxism is far more real to my imagination, and true to my experience, than a Marxism that seeks the aid of Christianity."[24] It is easy to see that other Communists, Christians, Socialists, and pacifists might find it hard to agree with Murry, especially when one could never be sure at what time Murry, the ally, would become the opponent. The resulting confusion was aptly expressed by G. K. Chesterton in a radio review of *William Blake*. He described Murry as "the voice of one crying in the wilderness: 'There is no God, and Marx is His prophet.' "[25]

One might find a virtue in this variability in that Murry, by joining movements and disproving them "on his pulses," was doing a service in exposing them. Philip Mairet, for example, notes that Murry's "temporary adoption of 'communism' in the *Adelphi* amounted to an innocent, and socially valuable betrayal of a bad cause."[26] Nevertheless, there is justice in an opposing argument that an intuitive and passively "open" approach, which works well in allowing the critic to appreciate and reveal the beauties of literature, is at a disadvantage in books demanding urgent social action. As one reads through Murry's books of social criticism over the twenty-five-year period—*The Fallacy of Economics* (1932), *The Necessity of Communism* (1932), *The Necessity of Pacifism* (1937), *The Defence of Democracy* (1939), *The Price of Leadership* (1939), *The Betrayal of Christ by the Churches* (1940), *Christocracy* (1942), *Adam and Eve* (1944), *The Free Society* (1948) and *Love, Freedom and Society* (1957)—one tends to lose faith because each book is too quickly *passé.* The knowledge that a book, with all its dialectic and arguments for action, is a step in a somewhat emotional (although undoubtedly sincere) personal search and that the dialectic and arguments as such are soon to be revised and perhaps contradicted in an ensuing book weakens belief in the pattern of reasoning within each book.

Murry's social and political career has the appearance of a changing dialogue in which he believed in one side at a time. Insofar as he was a man of action, Murry seemed to lack what might be called "the sense of vow"—that a course once taken carries responsibilities. No doubt the thoughtful and sensitive person needs to reconsider the nature of his commitment from time to time, but Murry was able to change course frequently without, apparently, feeling a great awareness of the responsibility for past action—an awareness associated with the phrase "breaking one's vow." If there is not this "sense of vow," other people involved in the social action have some justification for feeling that they have been "used," that they are but an "experience" in the subjective journey of their colleague or, more seriously, "guide."

Yet, despite the disturbing changes in viewpoint and the frequent looseness in language, there is in these books a central theme—a general atmosphere or tone more than a theme perhaps—which ultimately is more important than the arguments. Murry, in the tradition of Carlyle and Ruskin, insists that society should be morally and not acquisitively based and that social organization must be determined by the will of good men. It is dangerously fatal in a technological age for men to allow themselves to drift with a sense of helplessness, feeling that the machine and the organization direct, rather than that men do. Like Ruskin, Murry was acutely aware of the dangers of the machine age—in fact, much of his theorizing bears a close resemblance to Ruskin's *Unto This Last* except that Murry emphasized the need to incorporate rather than abolish the machine. Particularly interesting in this group of works is *The Price of Leadership,* in which the ideas of Coleridge and Arnold are developed in support of Murry's conviction that only a genuinely Christian ruling class would enable democracy to continue.

From his own struggles with the social organization, Murry issued a book of his experiences entitled *Community Farm* (1952). A very readable, relaxed—sometimes humorous—book, it is different in tone from his early autobiography, *Between Two Worlds*. He is no longer anxiously suspended between two worlds; he is settled, happily ruminative. He has, in a sense, come back to his first love, which almost literally, is the soil of England: "England's first duty to the world society is to be England.... And one of the simplest and safest ways of helping to ensure that it shall be England and not the hardware section of the world department store is for Englishmen to cultivate to the full the land that has been given them for an inheritance."[27]

II *Final Essays*

As those who knew him well have testified, one of Murry's outstanding qualities was his unflagging energy. He was able to produce his astonishing number of books and articles—as well as lecture, broadcast, reread Greek and Latin Classics, and revise his scholarship on Keats and Shakespeare—in any circumstance, however trying. In the last decade of his life, achieving domestic happiness and financial security, he was due for a period of relaxation. In a way he did relax—his writing has a more relaxed tone—but he did not stop writing; in fact, he was grateful for the chance to write "unprofessional" essays "to please myself."

Having worked out his ideas on religion and politics, he then returned to literary criticism that was "uncontaminated (and uninspired)," he wrote in an extreme moment, "by any effort to save my soul, by discovering what I do, or ought to, believe."[28] The most substantial outcome of this determination was *Jonathan Swift* (1954). For the rest, he wrote essays and broadcast talks, some of which were collected in *Looking Before and After* (1948); *Katherine Mansfield and Other Literary Portraits* (1949); *The Conquest of Death* (1951—discussed in Chapter 6); *Unprofessional Essays* (1956); *Love, Freedom and Society* (1957); and, published posthumously, *Katherine Mansfield and Other Literary Studies* (1959).

The choice of Swift for a major work was less surprising than Murry himself seemed to think. He chose Swift, he said, as "a sort of challenge to myself—to write a book on someone with whom I could not *possibly* identify myself" because the personage was "the very antipodes of myself."[29] It would have been more correct to say "someone who was the 'antipodes' of the 'save-my-soul' *part* of myself." We have noted in Chapter 2 and elsewhere that there were two basic elements in Murry's psychological composition: the mystical and the Classical, the Classical becoming almost Johnsonian at times. Swift satisfied this second element; in fact, Swift must have been intriguing to Murry in several ways because he touched Murry at a number of points—sometimes by being, at least on the surface, completely opposite.

To begin with, Murry had always tried to find the genuinely right path in life for himself and society; and, having quite frequently thought he had found it, he declared it with an open and confessional change of heart. Swift, though equally concerned with personal salvation and social justice, was secretive, "a man of masks." Swift would never have been capable of the confessional autobiography that Murry wrote. Similarly, Murry must have been intrigued by a man who could be so greatly successful as a writer but who had made a "hash" of the man-woman love relationship. The spirit of *Adam and Eve* was as foreign to Swift as could be imagined, in view of his treatment of Vanessa and Stella (incidentally, Murry seems to be overconfident that there was a secret marriage here) and of his growing disgust of physical, especially feminine, humanity. Then, as Murry points out, Swift, who avoided children, produced what is, in one aspect, a most successful children's book—*Gulliver's Travels*—and wrote to Stella in baby language.

There are also notable similarities. In style, Swift was almost a perfect example of the principles of sincerity and precision which had been laid down in *The Problem of Style;* and, like Murry, Swift is concerned with conduct on the basis of rational, moral, and human values—the Christian Classicist (a similarity which recalls Murry's enthusiastic support of Irving Babbitt). Reason for Swift was based on a religious mystery; Murry goes so far as to observe that his concept of reason was "almost mystical"—it was "akin to the Platonic intuition of the Good."[30] Like Murry, Swift also went through political battles with men of affairs, knew political changes and the mixture of ideals and economics, of theory and expediency, the tussle of war and peace.

Murry uses the critical approach he used in his earlier books on great writers: that of the "poetic life." In the preface, he states that his "aim has been to write a book which should be at once a life of Swift and a critical study of his works." He is aware that "the combination is not very fashionable nowadays," but he is unrepentant in believing that "the study of [a great writer's] life and work do fructify each other, and that to hold them vigorously apart is, very often, to refuse illumination."[31] Although some critics made the objection which Murry had foreseen—one called the book "unsophisticated"—the critical reception was generally good, a fact which seemed suspicious to some of Murry's supporters. A particularly good review appeared in *The Times Literary Supplement,* very fittingly since Murry had learned much of his craft in working for that journal.

As might have been expected, Murry excelled in the intuitive illumination of works obviously and closely related to Swift's personal experience, such as the early poems. As *The Times* reviewer said, "Nobody has as yet written so judicious and understanding a study of Swift's youthful pindarics and rhyming poems as Mr. Middleton Murry."[32] Murry refers to the six early attempts at verse as poems of "self-description." As he often did in starting an analysis, Murry sets a question: Why did Swift in 1694 willingly leave Temple's service and abandon his ambitions? Murry demonstrates that, in spite of the conventional style, there is an "emotional nakedness" about the poems. The young Swift believes that to write good poetry, the poet must believe in moral beauty; and this moral beauty is identified with Sir William Temple. In the first five poems, this is the constant theme, except one to Dr. William Sancroft; and even here Temple outshines the saintly Sancroft. But in the sixth poem, "Occasioned by Sir William Temple's Illness and Recovery," Swift says farewell to his poetic muse and to Temple. Temple had repulsed him; the man whom Swift had seen as father had rejected him. In this literary and emotional crisis, he turns on his muse and parts from an "extreme angry" Sir William.[33]

Also in line with Murry's earlier work—his *Keats,* for example —he gives a great deal of attention to the female influence on

Swift. He explores the relationships with Stella and Vanessa, and he applies his previous studies of the man-woman relation (in *Adam and Eve* particularly) to Swift's work. In the chapter on " 'Gulliver': The Personal Equation," Murry, in treating of Swift's disgust with the Yahoos, cannot escape "the notion that Swift is engaged in annihilating Stella herself as a sexual being." Swift saves "Stella from becoming a Yahoo, as she would like to have been."*

No doubt Murry's own experience of the literary man in politics and government ministries helped to make his presentation of Swift in the milieu of his time one of the most valuable parts of the book: "The chapters occupied with Swift's services to the Tory Ministry, his association with Harley and St. John, and his superb achievements as a political pamphleteer, are perhaps the best part of Mr. Middleton Murry's book. It is all admirably done. His characterization of notabilities, his setting of the scene of intrigue, cabal and manoeuvre for position, could hardly be bettered; and he has done Harley good service in according him the gifts and virtues he possessed."[34]

As a footnote, one critic pays tribute to Murry's sensitive reading of "A Letter of Advice to a Young Poet." Murry regards this document as unsatisfactory because parts of it read like clever imitations of Swift by somebody else. From the critic's own researches, he had come to the conclusion this is "exactly what they are."[35] The instance demonstrates that, whatever his other interests, Murry never lost his gift of extreme sensitivity to the written word.

The last essays that Murry wrote were published in *Unprofessional Essays* and in *Katherine Mansfield and Other Literary Studies,* the only exception being the one on Katherine Mansfield, which was based on a lecture given in the United States in 1935. Although Murry published her letters and journals (in the belief that the world should have all her "legacy of truth"), he wrote little criticism on her. In *Katherine Mansfield and*

---

* In his influential *Life Against Death* (Middletown, Conn., 1959) Norman O. Brown borrows Murry's phrase "the excremental vision" for a chapter heading, but opposes Murry's interpretation of this aspect of Swift's life.

Other Literary Portraits, he answered some points made by V. S. Pritchett and argued that it was mistaken to classify her art with that of Virginia Woolf;[36] but in the essay based on the 1935 lecture, he examines her work more closely. He emphasizes her "peculiar gift of *spontaneity*" and her ardent desire for experience through which she was able to probe "the ground pattern of her life and work": "the conflict between Love and Disillusion." From her works, as well as from his own knowledge of her as her husband, he demonstrates how her bitter revulsions from life were followed by periods of loving acceptance.[37]

Understandably overrating her, he put her in an early comment in a class with Chekhov: "I think that of all the writers of my generation Katherine Mansfield had by far the deepest (because the most instinctive) understanding of Tchehov. There was some personal bond between them, such that though Tchehov was dead, some essential communication seemed to pass between his spirit and hers. He was always living to her, always at her elbow to remind her of the necessity of that strange purity of soul which they shared."[38]

The final essays, though quieter and more leisured in tone, reveal that Murry did not, over the years, change his basic critical approach. There is the same earnest amateur quality, and the anti-specialist, catholic spread. Thus, in these essays, he criticizes three novelists—Henry Fielding, George Gissing, and Henry Williamson—of three succeeding centuries; a modern verse playwright, T. S. Eliot; and an American poet of a century ago, Walt Whitman. However, in one way or another the essays deal with his main concern in the last years: the achievement of a state of love centered on a satisfying man-woman relationship. In the essay on Fielding,[39] for example, he takes Dr. Leavis to task for depreciating Fielding by claiming that the novelist did not have the "intense moral preoccupation" which Leavis demands of those in "the great tradition." Murry, who effectively expounds the serious purpose behind Fielding's work, gives a new layer of meaning to the comedy of affairs. The key word is "generosity," and Murry sees in *Tom Jones* especially a masterpiece in its insight into "generosity of soul" and "generosity of body." Murry maintained his critical ability to revive the deeper significance of commonly used words. He used "generosity" as the title of his last broadcast for the British Broadcasting Company in November 1956, ranging from the "most generous" Hamlet through the application of the word to Fielding and Dickens.

As for Gissing,[40] Murry sees him as the portrayer of the "demonic female," the one incapable of generosity. The dangerous type is not so much the outright shrew as "la femme moyenne," an increasingly common phenomenon in modern society, whom Gissing called the "shop-girl" type, who brings a sense of career and her particular, conscious goals into marriage. Gissing himself had a sad marital experience which Murry, until he had come through to his final happiness with his fourth wife, could sympathize with. But perhaps, like Gissing, he would not have had it otherwise; his productive power, as he says of Gissing's, was probably "the direct effect of an escape from suffering that was personally intolerable, though creatively stimulating."

Since Murry was no longer writing for income, he tended to be more expansive in his last essays, especially in quoting. One could always depend on him to have thoroughly read the work under discussion and to have an uncanny knack of picking out the right passages for quotation. His final essay on Henry Williamson[41] is to a large extent an introductory essay with many specimens of Williamson's work. However, it achieved its purpose: several critics, in reviewing this essay, have expressed their intention to read Williamson's latest work—just what Murry intended to accomplish. Many writers have cause to be grateful to Murry for this ability of his. He achieves his end not by mere eulogizing but by a balanced appraisal, in which literature is the real test. Thus he admits that Williamson was justly blamed for his pro-Hitler sympathies, but he convinces the reader that Williamson is a literary artist who draws his characters "with such loving sympathy and such firmness of imaginative outline that we are entirely absorbed by their vicissitudes."

At the same time, he was still unable to put an esthetic distance between himself and T. S. Eliot. In his criticism of Eliot's plays,[42] he cannot avoid a concentration on Eliot's "occlusion of human love." The Murry of *Adam and Eve* is repelled by the choice of "ascetic vocation on the one hand and unloving marriage on the other"; and Murry the mystic resents "a kind of religious mysticism ... which has little use for the familiar things of earth and little sympathy with the struggles, the delights and the achievements of more ordinary folk." So far, many would align themselves with Murry's objection; but he presses it in a logical analysis which—somewhat in the manner of Thomas Rymer—tends to ignore the poetry and symbolism of a poetic play's development: "Harry has at last consented to the death of his wife. Did he push her overboard? Did he only imagine that he pushed her? That is left perplexingly vague. Equally important is an answer to the question: Is there a real and causal connection between Harry's father's desire to kill Amy, and Harry's impulse to kill his wife?" So Murry drills away, rather as Eliot did years before at "the inner voice."

With Eliot as with Lawrence there was, for Murry, an impasse on the question of the true man-woman relationship. When Murry was writing the essay on Eliot's plays, he apparently saw himself "as representing something in between T. S. Eliot and D. H. Lawrence."[43] But there is a question whether one can place oneself "between" geniuses in the way that Murry suggests. Murry came nearer to defining his true position when, in the course of the essay, he referred to the attempt to "interpret" one of Eliot's plays "from an ordinarily human standpoint."

Temperamentally, Murry was much more at home with Whitman, the "poet-prophet of democracy."[44] In fact, there is such obvious sympathy between writer and subject in this essay that one wonders whether Murry considered himself, on the prophetic side at least, as the modern Whitman. There is a parallel in the details of their experiences—the basic mystical experience, for example, followed by a lifetime articulation of the insight that this gave: "the *Song of Myself* rightly considered, is the explication of an eternal moment." Like Keats, Whitman treats the world as "a Vale of Soul-making" in which man learns his deepest lessons through personal "explorative experience," the "I" of the poems. Whitman looks forward to the new democracy, the kind of state which Murry describes in his book *The Free Society*; moreover, Whitman bases this new democracy on the inner conscience, on a "true and generous" relationship of the sexes, and on a sense of beauty in the organization of society as well as in art.

"Christianity and Tragedy,"[45] the closing essay in *Love, Freedom and Society,* the last of his books to be published in Murry's lifetime is a fitting conclusion to Murry's intellectual and spiritual journey. Murry feels that he has developed a practical synthesis "beyong the prophets" (referring in particular to Lawrence and Schweitzer). In a way, he returns to two old traditions, but in their union he sees an ascension to a new truth. His proposed synthesis resolves Murry's basic delimmas through the union of Classic tragedy and Christian mystery, and in the harmony beyond the pain of experience; the spiritual vision of the great literary artists is made real in personal and social history; and there is a final integration of "body" and "soul."

"Christian tragedy," Murry maintains, is possible in the modern context of lack of belief in the supernatural, as it has not been before. Tragedy died out in the traditional medieval view of Christianity since the good man could only go to heaven. But with the humanist view of Christ, tragedy is not only possible; it is an advance on Classic tragedy. It is no longer "an unavailing struggle of the hero with Fate, or Destiny, conceived as a dark mysterious power beyond the gods"; it has become, with the transformation through Christian consciousness, "essentially the tragedy of human freedom, and human character, struggling against the inertia and evil in man." Shakespeare shows this transition from the Greek, one result of this tradition being his emphasis on love. Christ is the perfect consummation; tragedy comes into human history as the supreme sacrifice of love.

Just as, early in his career, Murry demanded a return to Aristotle at the same time that he was expressing his mystical approach to criticism,[46] so now he turns to Aristotle to explain the tragedy of Christ. "From one aspect, our experience of the tragedy of Jesus is an illumination of Aristotle's perplexity" over the meaning of "catharsis." Man's sympathy of love and his awe before the mystery are a heightening of Aristotle's attempt to define the experience: "The pity and terror are heightened to love and awe and the purification of them (which we also experience) is transcended into a sense of revelation."

With Christ as the archetypal tragic figure, the imagination of Murry the literary critic and the experience of Murry the mystic are indissolubly one:

My imaginative experience of Jesus is at once unique and not unique among my spiritual experiences. Something like it happens to me when I contemplate the life and death of John Keats, when I read the *Agamemnon* or the *Persae* or *Hamlet* or *King Lear,* when I think faithfully of D. H. Lawrence, when I read Blake's *Milton* or Constant's *Adolphe:* I could make a whole curious catalogue of such experiences. Yet, for some reason, they all blend into and find a focal point in my experience of Jesus. The only satisfying symbolization of this peculiar happening I have ever found is in Blake's doctrine of the Divine Humanity, whereby, in the realm of Imagination, which (Blake says) "is the human existence itself," all is united in "the Divine Humanity, the one Man, even Jesus."

Tragedy and love, then, are "inseparably bound together" in the fact of Christ. But one more question remains to be answered: If the story of Christ is tragedy brought into actual history, who is the "artist" of this tragedy? Not "God"—this is too simple—but Christ Himself, since love is evolutionary of itself. Murry maintains the organic and biological metaphor to the end.

Ultimately, Murry had "found out for himself." Although in the course of his "life-adventure" he exasperated many people, yet he helped many to "find themselves"—including some, like D. H. Lawrence, whom he had exasperated. Not greatly inventive, he had a mind characterized by a sense of discovery; appropriately, he called a collection of his essays *Discoveries.* He was an outstanding editor, able to recognize the original and valuable, not only in his contemporaries, but also in minor and often half-forgotten talents of the past. Particularly in the days of disillusionment in the early 1920's, he performed a great service in keeping alive a positive and creative literary spirit.

Throughout his life, he did as much as any critic and journalist to make the average man aware of the ideal in his cultural heritage. He could not, and would not, separate society, labor, and love of the soil from the visions of the great literary artists. As he said early in his career when staying with the farmer Thornhill: "Shakespeare and John Thornhill—they are England to me—'the heart of generosity.'" It is appropriate that on a gravestone in a small English country churchyard, Murry is described simply as "Author and Farmer."

[158]

Notes and References

Chapter One

1. "William Godwin," *Countries of the Mind: Second Series* (London, 1931), p. 181.
2. *Ibid.*
3. *Katherine Mansfield and Other Literary Studies* (London, 1959), p. viii.
4. "The Dream of a Queer Fellow," *The Evolution of an Intellectual* (London, 1920), p. 31.
5. *Discoveries* (London, 1924), pp. 106-107.
6. Quoted by F. A. Lea, *The Life of John Middleton Murry* (London, 1959), p. 7.
7. *Adam and Eve* (London, 1944), p. 37.
8. *Between Two Worlds* (London, 1935), p. 109.
9. *The Things We Are* (London, 1922), p. 195.
10. *The Free Society* (London, 1948), p. 112.
11. *God: An Introduction to the Science of Metabiology* (London, 1929), p. 26.
12. See below, Chap. 6.
13. The experience is described in *To the Unknown God* (London, 1924), pp. 42-44 and in *God*, pp. 35-36.
14. *The Life of John Middleton Murry*, p. 305.
15. Margaret Tims, *The Aryan Path*, XXXI, 1 (January 1960), p. 34.
16. *Poems: 1916-1920* (London, 1921), p. 55.
17. *Still Life* (London, 1916), pp. 22-23.
18. *The Things We Are*, pp. 24-25.
19. *The Collected Letters of D. H. Lawrence*, ed. Harry T. Moore, 2 vols., (New York, 1962), I, 238.
20. *The Critic in Judgment or Belshazzar of Barons Court* (London, 1919).
21. *Cinnamon and Angelica* (London, 1920).
22. *Between Two Worlds*, pp. 368–69.
23. *Reminiscences of D. H. Lawrence* (London, 1933), p. 84.
24. *Fyodor Dostoevsky: A Critical Study* (London, 1916), p. v.

25. *Ibid.*, pp. 115–16.
26. *Ibid.*, p. 116.
27. *Ibid.*, p. 124.
28. *Ibid.*, pp. 118–19.
29. *Ibid.*, p. 140.
30. *Ibid.*, p. 201.
31. *Ibid.*, pp. 162–63.
32. *Ibid.*, p. 164.
33. *Ibid.*, p. 184.
34. *Ibid.*, p. 196.
35. *Ibid.*, p. 249.
36. *Ibid.*, p. 213.
37. *Ibid.*, p. 250.
38. *Ibid.*, p. 219.
39. *Ibid.*, p. 253.
40. *Ibid.*, p. 259.
41. Quoted by F. A. Lea, *The Life of John Middleton Murry*, p. 38.
42. *Between Two Worlds*, p. 316.
43. *Ibid.*, p. 314.
44. *The Collected Letters of D. H. Lawrence*, I, 469–70.
45. Dorothy Brewster, *East-West Passage* (London, 1954), p. 162.
46. "Realism," *The Evolution of an Intellectual*, p. 91.
47. *The Evolution of an Intellectual*, pp. 155–65.
48. "The Nature of Civilisation," *The Evolution of an Intellectual*, p. 173.
49. *The Evolution of an Intellectual*, pp. 16–29.
50. *Ibid.*, pp. 30–38.
51. *Ibid.*, p. 17.
52. *Ibid.*
53. *Ibid.*, p. 33.
54. *Ibid.*, p. 29.

Chapter Two

1. "The Nature of Poetry," *Discoveries* (London, 1924), pp. 13–14.
2. "The Function of Criticism," *Aspects of Literature* (London, 1920), pp. 7, 9.
3. "On Reading Novels," *Things to Come* (London, 1928), pp. 254-55.
4. Preface to "The Travellers' Library" edition of *The Evolution of an Intellectual* (London, 1927), pp. 9–10.
5. See below, p. 44.
6. *Reminiscences of D. H. Lawrence* (London, 1933), p. 262, and letter to Lady Morrell, *The Collected Letters of D. H. Lawrence*, ed. Harry T. Moore, 2 vols., (New York, 1962), II, 1124.

7. Introduction, *J. Middleton Murry: Selected Criticism 1916-1957*, ed. Richard Rees (London, 1960), p. vii.

8. *The London Magazine,* VII, 1 (January 1960), 65.

9. Karl Miller, "The Murry-Go-Round," *The Spectator,* January 8, 1960, p. 44.

10. "On Editing; and on Romanticism," *To the Unknown God* (London, 1924), p. 81. (I have used the essays originally appearing in *The Adelphi* and *The Criterion,* as published in the respective collections of essays in book form.)

11. *Ibid.,* p. 82.

12. "The Function of Criticism," *Selected Essays* (London, 1951), p. 27.

13. *To the Unknown God,* pp. 134–51.

14. *Ibid.,* p. 137.

15. *Ibid.,* p. 139.

16. *Ibid.,* p. 138.

17 "Shakespeare Criticism," *Aspects of Literature,* p. 200.

18. *To the Uknown God,* p. 141.

19. *Ibid.,* p. 84.

20. *Ibid.,* p. 148.

21. "Literature and Religion," *To the Unknown God,* pp. 179–80.

22. *Ibid.,* p. 180.

23. Foreword to J. Middleton Murry, *Katherine Mansfield and Other Literary Studies* (London, 1959), p. viii.

24. *Ibid.,* p. vii.

25. *Ibid.,* p. viii.

26. "Pure Poetry," *Countries of the Mind: Second Series* (London, 1931), p. 23.

27. "What is Style?" *Pencillings* (London, 1923), p. 101.

28. "The Poetry of Mr. Hardy," *Aspects of Literature,* p. 132.

29. See below, p. 52.

30. *Countries of the Mind: Second Series,* p. 25.

31. *The Adelphi,* III, 9 (February 1926), 585–95.

32. See in particular J. M. Murry, "Towards a Synthesis," *The Criterion,* V, iii (June 1927), 294–313; Ramon Fernandez, "A Note on Intelligence and Intuition," *The Criterion,* VI, iv (October 1927), 332–39; and T. S. Eliot, "Mr. Middleton Murry's Synthesis," *The Criterion,* VI, iv (October 1927), 340–47.

33. Quoted by Rayner Heppenstall, *John Middleton Murry: A Study in Excellent Normality* (London, 1934), p. 16.

34. Quoted in F. A. Lea, *The Life of John Middleton Murry* (London, 1959), p. 72.

35. "Mr. Eliot at Lambeth," *The Adelphi,* II, 1 (April 1931), 70–73.

36. Quoted in F. A. Lea, *The Life of John Middleton Murry,* p. 72.
37. *Ibid.,* pp. 91–92.
38. Northrop Frye, *Anatomy of Criticism* (Princeton, 1957), p. 19.
39. "Amiel," *Countries of the Mind* (London, 1922), p. 197.
40. See above, p. 40.
41. "The Function of Criticism," *Aspects of Literature,* pp. 4–5.
42. *Ibid.,* p. 6.
43. See below, p. 54.
44. First published in 1922. The edition here used is the easily available "Oxford Paperbacks" ed. first issued by the Oxford University Press, London, in 1960.
45. *Ibid.,* p. 7.
46. *Ibid.,* p. 37.
47. *Ibid.,* p. 13.
48. *Ibid.,* p. 72.
49. *Ibid.*
50. *Ibid.,* p. 25.
51. *Ibid.,* p. 31.
52. *Ibid.*
53. *Ibid.,* p. 69.
54. *Ibid.,* p. 79.
55. *Ibid.,* p. 85.
56. *Ibid.,* p. 84.
57. *Ibid.,* p. 100.
58. *Countries of the Mind: Second Series,* pp. 1–16.
59. *Ibid.,* p. 15.
60. "Literature and Religion," *To the Unknown God,* p. 164.
61. *The Problem of Style,* p. 118.
62. *Ibid.,* p. 123.
63. *Ibid.,* p. 16.
64. *Ibid.,* p. 118.
65. For example, see above, p. 31.
66. "Literature and Religion," *To the Unknown God,* pp. 167–68.
67. See Chapter 5.
68. "Coleridge's Criticism," *Aspects of Literature,* pp. 186–87.

Chapter Three

1. *Between Two Worlds* (London, 1935), pp. 192–93.
2. *Twentieth Century Authors,* ed. Kunitz and Haycraft (New York, 1942), p. 1002.
3. *Aspects of Literature* (London, 1920), pp. 15–28.
4. *Ibid.,* p. 25.

5. See below, p. 100.

6. *Aspects of Literature*, pp. 26–27.

7. "The Cry in the Wilderness," *Aspects of Literature*, p. 167.

8. *Ibid.*, p. 170.

9. *Ibid.*, pp. 170–71.

10. *Ibid.*, pp. 174–75.

11. *Ibid.*, p. 175.

12. "Baudelaire," *Countries of the Mind* (London, 1922), p. 160.

13. "Gustave Flaubert, 1821–1880," *Countries of the Mind*, pp. 206–207. For a possible explanation of Murry's view of Flaubert, see below, p. 74.

14. *Countries of the Mind*, pp. 154 and 156.

15. *Ibid.*, p. 157.

16. "Gotthold Ephraim Lessing," *Countries of the Mind: Second Series* (London, 1931), p. 142.

17. *Ibid.*, p. 144.

18. *Ibid.*, p. 143.

19. *Ibid.*, p. 147.

20. "The Poetry of Mr. Hardy," *Aspects of Literature*, p. 136.

21. *Ibid.*, p. 131.

22. "Mr. Yeats's Swan Song," *Aspects of Literature*, p. 40.

23. *Ibid.*, p. 45.

24. "Gerard Manley Hopkins," *Aspects of Literature*, p. 60.

25. *Ibid.*, p. 58.

26. *Ibid.*, p. 61.

27. *Heaven—and Earth* (London, 1938), p. 93.

28. "The Poetry of Edward Thomas," *Aspects of Literature*, p. 32.

29. *Ibid.*

30. *Ibid.*, p. 33.

31. "The Nostalgia of Mr. Masefield," *Aspects of Literature*, p. 156.

32. *Ibid.*, p. 151.

33. "Samuel Butler," *Aspects of Literature*, p. 109.

34. "The Poetry of John Clare," *Countries of the Mind*, pp. 101–19; "The Case of John Clare," *Discoveries*, 2nd ed. (London, 1930), pp. 205–15.

35. "The Countess of Winchelsea," *Countries of the Mind: Second Series*, pp. 166–80.

36. *Countries of the Mind*, p. 106.

37. *Ibid.*, p. 114.

38. *Ibid.* p. 115.

39. *Unprofessional Essays* (London, 1956), pp. 53–111.

40. "The Poetry of William Collins," *Countries of the Mind*, p. 85.

41. *Ibid.*, p. 94.

42. *Ibid.*, p. 84.

43. See below, p. 67.

44. "The Poetry of Walter de la Mare," *Countries of the Mind,* pp. 132–33.

45. *Ibid.*, p. 130.

46. *Countries of the Mind: Second Series,* pp. 63–77.

47. *Ibid.*, p. 74.

48. *Ibid.*, p. 69.

49. "English Poetry in the Eighteenth Century," *Discoveries,* p. 163.

50. *Ibid.*, p. 173.

51. "On the Madness of Christopher Smart," *Discoveries,* p. 186.

52. "Thomas Flatman," *Countries of the Mind: Second Series,* p. 165.

53. "The Countess of Winchelsea," *Countries of the Mind: Second Series,* p. 174.

54. *Ibid.*, p. 171.

55. *"Arabia Deserta," Countries of the Mind,* p. 145.

56. "English Prose in the Nineteenth Century," *Discoveries,* p. 217.

57. "On Reading Novels," *Things to Come* (London, 1928), p. 250.

58. "The Break-up of the Novel," *Discoveries,* p. 148.

59. "Novels and Thought-Adventures," *To the Unknown God* (London, 1924), p. 128.

60. *Ibid.*, p. 129.

61. *Discoveries,* p. 144.

62. *Ibid.*, p. 147.

63. *Ibid.*, p. 151.

64. See above, pp. 39.

65. "Stendhal," *Countries of the Mind,* p. 229.

66. *Ibid.*, p. 234.

67. *Ibid.*

68. *Ibid.*, p. 235.

69. *The Problem of Style,* Oxford Paperbacks ed. (London, 1960), p. 15.

70. "Marcel Proust," *Discoveries,* p. 118.

71. *Ibid.*, p. 115.

72. *Ibid.*, p. 121.

73. *Ibid.*, p. 126.

74. *Ibid.*, p. 127.

75. *Ibid.*, pp. 121–22.

76. "The Wisdom of Anatole France," *Aspects of Literature,* p. 48.

77. *Ibid.*

78. *Ibid.*

79. *Ibid.*, p. 51.

80. "Gustave Flaubert," *Countries of the Mind,* pp. 207-208.

81. *Ibid.*, p. 206.

82. *Ibid.*, p. 207.

83. *Ibid.*, p. 221.

84. "Flaubert and Flaubart," *Discoveries,* pp. 287-314. There is strong—even emotional—rebuttal to Murry's comments on E. E. Cummings in *The Dial* LXXVI, 4 (April 1924), 376–79.

85. *Countries of the Mind*, p. 217.

86. *Ibid.*, p. 220.

87. *Ibid.*, p. 221.

88. *Ibid.*, p. 211.

89. *Ibid.*, p. 212.

90. *Ibid.*

91. "Thoughts on Tchehov," *Aspects of Literature*, pp. 78–79.

92. "Anton Tchehov," *Discoveries*, p. 91.

93. "The Significance of Russian Literature," *Discoveries*, pp. 70–73.

94. *Ibid.*, p. 48.

95. *Ibid.*, p. 52.

96. "Jacques-Bénigne Bossuet," *Countries of the Mind: Second Series,* pp. 126–40.

97. "Amiel," *Countries of the Mind,* pp. 186–87.

98. "Amiel's Love Story," *Countries of the Mind: First Series,* new ed. rev. and enlarged (London, 1931), p. 157.

Chapter Four

1. *Shakespeare* (London, 1936), p. 411.

2. *Keats and Shakespeare* (London, 1925), p. 4.

3. *Between Two Worlds* (London, 1935), p. 446.

4. *The Nation and Athenaeum*, XXXVII (September 26, 1925), 766.

5. *The Manchester Guardian,* March 18, 1955, p. 6.

6. E. M. W. Tillyard, *The Miltonic Setting* (London, 1938), p. 29.

7. *Keats and Shakespeare*, p. 41.

8. *Ibid.*, p. 32.

9. *Ibid.*, pp. 34–38

10. *Ibid.*, pp. 45–47.

11. *Ibid.*, p. 48.

12. "Keats and Milton," *Keats* (London, 1955), p. 266.

13. *Keats and Shakespeare*, p. 58.

14. *Ibid.*, p. 63.

15. *Ibid.*, pp. 65–66.

16. *Ibid.*, p. 55.

17. *Ibid.*, Ch. VI.

18. *Ibid.*, p. 75.

19. *Ibid.*
20. *Ibid.*, p. 77.
21. *Ibid.*, p. 76.
22. *Ibid.*, pp. 229–30.
23. *Ibid.*, p. 70.
24. *Ibid.*, p. 87.
25. *Ibid.*, p. 92.
26. *Ibid.*, p. 109.
27. *Ibid.*, p. 111.
28. *Ibid.*, p. 122.
29. *Ibid.*, p. 124.
30. *Ibid.*, p. 125.
31. *Ibid.*, pp. 130–32.
32. Quoted in F. A. Lea, *The Life of John Middleton Murry* (London, 1959), p. 128.
33. *Keats and Shakespeare,* p. 142.
34. *Ibid.*, pp. 140–41.
35. *Ibid.*, p. 146.
36. *Ibid.*, p. 147.
37. *Ibid.*, p. 157.
38. *Ibid.*, p. 159.
39. *Ibid.*, p. 169.
40. *Ibid.*, p. 168.
41. *Ibid.*, p. 175.
42. *Ibid.*, p. 214.
43. *Keats,* p. 13.
44. *Ibid.*, pp. 145–65.
45. *Katherine Mansfield and Other Literary Portraits* (London, 1949), pp. 39–40.
46. *Keats,* p. 292.
47. *Ibid.*, pp. 269–91.
48. *The Miltonic Setting* (London, 1938), pp. 29–30.
49. *Keats,* p. 251.
50. *Ibid.*, p. 293.
51. *Ibid.*, pp. 252–54.
52. *Ibid.*, p. 266.
53. *Ibid.*, pp. 267–68.
54. *Ibid.*, pp. 211–12.
55. *Ibid.*, p. 217.
56. *Ibid.*, p. 218.
57. *Ibid.*, p. 225.
58. *Ibid.*, p. 299.
59. *Poems of John Keats* (London, 1926), p. 584.

60. *Keats*, pp. 238–249.

61. *Scrutiny*, IV, 4 (March 1936), 377. "Keats" also appears in the volume of Leavis' essays, *Revaluation*.

62. Dorothy Hewlett, *Adonais: A Life of John Keats* (New York, 1938), p. 174.

63. Aileen Ward, *John Keats: The Making of a Poet* (New York, 1963), p. 436.

64. Walter Jackson Bate, *John Keats* (Cambridge, Mass., 1963), p. 221.

65. E. C. Pettet, *On the Poetry of Keats* (Cambridge, England, 1957), p. 14.

66. *Ibid.*, pp. 207–208.

67. *Ibid.*, p. 352.

68. *Adam and Eve* (London, 1944), p. 127.

69. *The Challenge of Schweitzer* (London, 1948), p. 51.

70. Ronald G. B. Gorell, *John Keats: The Principle of Beauty* (London, 1948).

Chapter Five

1. Quoted in F. A. Lea, *The Life of John Middleton Murry* (London, 1959), p. 332.

2. *Community Farm* (London, 1952), p. 151.

3. "The Supremacy of Thomas Hardy," *The New Adelphi*, I, 3 (March 1928), 224.

4. *Heaven—and Earth* (London, 1938), pp. 62–63.

5. *Ibid.*, p. 65.

6. *Ibid.*, p. 76.

7. *Ibid.*, p. 109.

8. *Ibid.*, p. 87.

9. *Ibid.*, p. 117.

10. *Ibid.*, p. 106.

11. *Ibid.*, p. 107.

12. *Ibid.*, p. 170.

13. *Ibid.*, p. 161.

14. Quoted in *The Life of John Middleton Murry*, p. 340.

15. *Heaven—and Earth*, p. 195.

16. *Ibid.*, p. 201.

17. *Ibid.*, p. 207.

18. *Ibid.*, pp. 230–31.

19. *Ibid.*, p. 227.

20. *Ibid.*, p. 249.

21. *Ibid.*, p. 252.

22. *Ibid.*, p. 268.

23. *Ibid.*, p. 279.

24. *Ibid.*, p. 302.

25. *Ibid.*, p. 304.

26. *Ibid.*, p. 321.

27. *Ibid.*, p. 325.

28. *Ibid.*, p. 344.

29. *Ibid.*, p. 347.

30. *Ibid.*, p. 374.

31. *Ibid.*, p. 375.

32. *Ibid.*, p. 366.

33. *Ibid.*

34. *Ibid.*, p. 375.

35. *Shakespeare* (London, 1936), p. 39.

36. *Ibid.*, pp. 37–38.

37. Edward A. Armstrong, *Shakespeare's Imagination* (London, 1946), p. 156.

38. *Shakespeare,* p. 34.

39. *Shakespeare's History Plays* (London, 1944), p. 227.

40. *The Times (London) Literary Supplement*, February 8, 1936, p. 101.

41. "J. Middleton Murry," *Of Books and Humankind*, ed. John Butt (London, 1964), pp. 149–63.

42. *Ibid.*, and *The Imperial Theme*, 3rd ed. (London, 1951), pp. v–vi.

43. *Shakespeare's Problem Plays* (London, 1950), p. 15. On the subject of *Hamlet*, there is an interesting exchange of views between Murry and Wilson Knight in *The Adelphi (New Series)*, I, 4 (January 1931), pp. 341–47 and I, 5 (February 1931), pp. 426–28. In the course of his remarks, Murry observes that Melville's *Pierre* is "the profoundest of all commentaries on *Hamlet*."

44. G. Wilson Knight, *The Sovereign Flower* (London, 1958), p. 226.

45. *The Adelphi,* XII, 1 (April 1936), p. 59.

46. *Shakespeare,* pp. 356–57.

47. *Ibid.*, pp. 76–79.

48. *Ibid.*, p. 85.

49. *Ibid.*, p. 15.

50. See above, p. 108.

51. *Shakespeare,* p. 291.

52. *Ibid.*, pp. 291–92.

53. *Ibid.*, p. 94.

54. *Ibid.*, pp. 104–105.

55. *Ibid.*, p. 135.

56. *Ibid.,* p. 155.

57. *Ibid.,* p. 156.

58. *Ibid.,* p. 170.

59. *Ibid.,* p. 180.

60. *Ibid.,* p. 183.

61. *Ibid.,* p. 229.

62. *Ibid.,* p. 232.

63. *Ibid.,* p. 164.

64. Francis Fergusson, *The Idea of a Theater* (Princeton, 1949), p. 37.

65. *Shakespeare,* p. 189.

66. "The Theme of the Three Caskets" (1913) translated by C. M. J. Hubback and published in Sigmund Freud, *On Creativity and the Unconscious* (New York, 1958), pp. 63–75.

67. *Shakespeare,* p. 325.

68. "Hamlet," *Selected Essays* (New York, 1932), p. 121.

69. *Ibid.,* p. 402.

70. *Ibid.,* p. 396.

71. *Ibid.,* p. 411.

72. "Problems of the Shakespeare Sonnets," *Countries of the Mind: Second Series* (London, 1931), pp. 113–25.

73. *John Clare and Other Studies* (London, 1950).

74. *Ibid.,* pp. 31–44.

75. "The Creation of Falstaff," *John Clare and Other Studies,* pp. 181–207.

76. "Coriolanus," *John Clare and Other Studies,* pp. 222–45.

77. *John Clare and Other Studies,* pp. 45–57.

78. *Ibid.,* pp. 246–52.

79. *The Problem of Style,* Oxford Paperbacks ed. (London, 1960), pp. 103–104.

80. "Metaphor," *Countries of the Mind: Second Series,* pp. 1–16.

81. "The Nature of Poetry," *Discoveries* (London, 1924), p. 32.

82. *Ibid.*

83. *Ibid.,* p. 25.

84. *Ibid.,* p. 23.

85. *Ibid.,* pp. 38–40.

86. *Ibid.,* p. 44.

87. *Ibid.,* p. 19.

Chapter Six

1. *The Collected Letters of D. H. Lawrence,* ed. Harry T. Moore, 2 vols., (New York, 1962), I, 402.

2. *Ibid.,* II, 1154.

3. *Ibid.,* I, 321.

4. *Between Two Worlds* (London, 1935), p. 305.

5. *The Collected Letters of D. H. Lawrence,* I, 321. As Murry's biographer observes, Lawrence was later to refer to this novel: "It is the kind of wriggling self-abuse I can't make head or tail of." *Ibid.,* I, 492.

6. *Ibid.,* I, 394–96.

7. *Ibid.,* I, 440.

8. *Ibid.,* I, 441.

9. *Between Two Worlds,* p. 409.

10. *Ibid.,* p. 416.

11. Quoted in Beatrice Lady Glenavy, *Today We Will Only Gossip* (London, 1964), p. 193.

12. Quoted in F. A. Lea, *The Life of John Middleton Murry,* (London, 1959), p. 120.

13. *The Collected Letters of D. H. Lawrence,* II, 830.

14. *Ibid.,* II, 883, 886.

15. *Ibid.,* II, 1154.

16. *Reminiscences of D. H. Lawrence* (London, 1933), pp. 213–81.

17. *Ibid.,* p. 219.

18. *John Middleton Murry* (London, 1958), p. 26.

19. *D. H. Lawrence: Son of Woman,* with a new introduction (London, 1954), p. xvii.

20. *Reminiscences of D. H. Lawrence,* p. 18.

21. *Frieda Lawrence: The Memoirs and Correspondence,* ed. E. W. Tedlock (London, 1961), p. 367.

22. *D. H. Lawrence: Son of Woman,* pp. 388–89.

23. *Reminiscences of D. H. Lawrence,* p. 19.

24. E.g.: "You will not easily get a man to believe that his carnal love for the woman he has made his wife is as high a love as that he felt for his mother." *D. H. Lawrence: Son of Woman,* p. 21.

25. *Ibid.,* pp. 40–41.

26. *Ibid.,* pp. 118–19.

27. *Ibid.,* pp. 172–74.

28. *Ibid.,* p. 141.

29. *Ibid.,* p. 247.

30. *Ibid.,* p. 263.

31. *The Letters of D. H. Lawrence,* ed. with an intro. by Aldous Huxley (London, 1932), p. x.

32. Graham Hough, *The Dark Sun* (London, 1956), p. 13.

33. *Scrutiny,* I, 1 (May 1932), 27.

34. *Scrutiny,* XVII, 3 (Autumn 1950), 203.

35. *Love, Freedom and Society* (London, 1957), p. 56.

36. *D. H. Lawrence: Son of Woman,* pp. 337–38.

37. *D. H. Lawrence: Novelist* (New York, 1956), p. 298.

38. *Love, Freedom and Society*, p. 35.

39. *The Conquest of Death* (London, 1951).

40. *God: An Introduction to the Science of Metabiology* (London, 1929), p. 43.

41. *Ibid.*, pp. 260–66.

42. *William Blake* (London, 1933), p. 188.

43. *Ibid.*, p. 145.

44. *Ibid.*, p. 125.

45. *Adam and Eve: An Essay Towards a New and Better Society* (London, 1944), pp. 88–101.

46. See above, pp. 132-34.

47. *Love, Freedom and Society*, p. 79.

48. *Ibid.*, pp. 104–23.

49. Cf. George Seaver, *Albert Schweitzer: A Vindication—Being a Reply to "The Challenge of Schweitzer" by John Middleton Murry* (London, 1950).

50. *Love, Freedom and Society*, p. 201.

51. *Ibid.*, pp. 205–31.

52. See below, pp. 157-58.

53. Quoted in Harry T. Moore, *The Intelligent Heart: The Story of D. H. Lawrence* (New York, 1954), p. 226.

Chapter Seven

1. Quoted in F. A. Lea, *The Life of John Middleton Murry* (London, 1959), p. 110.

2. *Ibid.*, p. 332.

3. *The Aryan Path*, VI, 7 (July 1935), 446–50.

4. Quoted in *The Life of John Middleton Murry*, p. 345.

5. *The London Magazine*, IV, 5 (May 1957), 66–69.

6. See above, pp. 100-08.

7. Quoted in *The Life of John Middleton Murry*, p. 341.

8. T. R. Barnes, *Scrutiny*, II, 4 (March 1934), 424–26.

9. G. E. Bentley, Jr., and Martin K. Nurmi, *A Blake Bibliography* (Minneapolis, 1964), pp. 23–24.

10. Cf. F. A. Lea's comments on this aspect. *The Life of John Middleton Murry*, pp. 211–12.

11. *William Blake* (London, 1933), p. 316.

12. *The Necessity of Pacifism* (London, 1937), p. 26.

13. *William Blake*, p. 8.

14. *The Aryan Path*, V, 7 (July 1934) 462–66.

15. See comparison of Blake and Lawrence, above, p. 136.

16. *William Blake,* p. 107.

17. *Ibid.,* p. 214.

18. *Ibid.,* p. 218.

19. *Ibid.,* p. 254.

20. *The Aryan Path,* VII, 4 (April 1936), 192.

21. *God: An Introduction to the Science of Metabiology* (London, 1929), p. 113.

22. *The Life of Jesus* (London, 1926), pp. 115–16.

23. *Ibid.,* p. 129.

24. *The Defence of Democracy* (London, 1939), pp. 190, 203.

25. Quoted in Rayner Heppenstall, *Four Absentees* (London, 1960), p. 33.

26. *John Middleton Murry* (London, 1958), p. 33.

27. *Community Farm* (London, 1952), p. 151.

28. Quoted in *The Life of John Middleton Murry,* p. 340.

29. *Ibid.*

30. *Swift,* a pamphlet published for The British Council and the National Book League (London, 1955), p. 31.

31. *Jonathan Swift* (London, 1954), p. 9.

32. *The Times Literary Supplement,* April 16, 1954, p. 248.

33. *Jonathan Swift,* p. 53.

34. *The Times Literary Supplement,* April 16, 1954, p. 248.

35. Herbert Davis in *The Review of English Studies,* VI, 23 (1955), 319.

36. "The Isolation of Katherine Mansfield," *Katherine Mansfield and Other Literary Portraits* (London, 1949), pp. 7–15.

37. "Katherine Mansfield," *Katherine Mansfield and Other Literary Studies* (London, 1959), pp. 69–93.

38. From a review of books by Ivan Bunin. *The Dial,* LXXVI, 2 (February 1924), 194–95.

39. *Unprofessional Essays* (London, 1956), pp. 9–52.

40. *Katherine Mansfield and Other Literary Studies,* pp. 1–68.

41. *Ibid.,* pp. 95–162.

42. *Unprofessional Essays,* pp. 149–91.

43. Quoted in *The Life of John Middleton Murry,* p. 346.

44. *Unprofessional Essays,* pp. 113–48.

45. *Love, Freedom and Society* (London, 1957), pp. 232–253.

46. See above, pp. 40-41.

Selected Bibliography

PRIMARY SOURCES

1. *Works by Murry*

Fyodor Dostoevsky: A Critical Study. London: Secker, 1916. New York: Dodd, Mead, 1916. Boston: Small, Maynard, 1924.

Still Life. London: Constable, 1916. New York: Dutton, 1922.

The Critic in Judgment or Belshazzar of Barons Court. Richmond: Hogarth, 1919.

The Evolution of an Intellectual. London: Cobden-Sanderson, 1920. New York: Knopf, 1920. 2nd ed. London: Cape, 1927.

Cinnamon and Angelica. London: Cobden-Sanderson, 1920. 2nd ed. London: Dakers, 1941.

Aspects of Literature. London: Collins, 1920. New York: Knopf, 1920. 2nd ed. London: Cape, 1934.

Poems 1916-1920. London: Cobden-Sanderson, 1921.

The Problem of Style. London: Oxford University Press, 1922. Oxford Paperbacks ed., 1960.

Countries of the Mind. London: Collins, 1922. New York: Dutton, 1922. New ed. rev. and enlarged, London: Oxford University Press, 1931.

The Things We Are. London: Constable, 1922. New York: Dutton, 1922.

Pencillings. London: Collins, 1923. New York: Seltzer, 1925.

The Voyage. London: Constable, 1924.

To the Unknown God. London: Cape, 1924.

Discoveries. London: Collins, 1924. 2nd ed. London: Cape, 1930.

Keats and Shakespeare. London: Oxford University Press, 1925.

The Life of Jesus. London: Cape, 1926. American title: *Jesus, Man of Genius*. New York: Harper, 1926.

Things to Come. London: Cape, 1928. New York: Macmillan, 1928.

God: An Introduction to the Science of Metabiology. London: Cape, 1929. New York: Harper, 1929.

Studies in Keats. London: Oxford University Press, 1930.

D. H. Lawrence: Two Essays. Cambridge: Minority Press, 1930.

Countries of the Mind: Second Series. London: Oxford University Press, 1931. Issued with First Series, London: Oxford University Press, 1937.

Son of Woman: The Story of D. H. Lawrence. London: Cape, 1931. New York: Cape and Smith, 1931. *D. H. Lawrence: Son of Woman,* issued with a new intr. London: Cape, 1954.

The Necessity of Communism. London: Cape, 1932. New York: Seltzer, 1933.

The Fallacy of Economics. London: Faber and Faber, 1932.

The Wanderer. Larling: J. M. Murry, 12 issues, December 1933-November 1934.

The Life of Katherine Mansfield (with R. E. Mantz). London: Constable, 1933.

Reminiscences of D. H. Lawrence. London: Cape, 1933. New York: Holt, 1933.

William Blake. London: Cape, 1933. New York: McGraw-Hill, 1964.

Between Two Worlds. London: Cape, 1935. *The Autobiography of John Middleton Murry: Between Two Worlds.* New York: Messner, 1936.

Shakespeare. London: Cape, 1936. New York: Harcourt, Brace, 1936.

The Necessity of Pacifism. London: Cape, 1937.

The Pledge of Peace. London: H. Joseph, 1938.

Heaven—and Earth. London: Cape, 1938. American title: *Heroes of Thought.* New York: Messner, 1938.

Studies in Keats: New and Old. London: Oxford University Press, 1939.

The Defence of Democracy. London: Cape, 1939.

The Price of Leadership. London: S.C.M. Press, 1939. New York: Harper, 1939.

The Betrayal of Christ by the Churches. London: Dakers, 1940.

Christocracy. London: Dakers, 1942.

Adam and Eve. London: Dakers, 1944.

The Free Society. London: Dakers, 1948.

Looking Before and After. London: Sheppard Press, 1948.

The Challenge of Schweitzer. London: Jason Press, 1948.

Katherine Mansfield and Other Literary Portraits. London: Nevill, 1949.

The Mystery of Keats. London: Nevill, 1949.

John Clare and Other Studies. London: Nevill, 1950.

The Conquest of Death. London: Nevill, 1951.

Community Farm. London: Nevill, 1952.

Jonathan Swift. London: Cape 1954. New York: Noonday Press, 1955.

Swift. (Pamphlet published for The British Council and the National Book League.) London: Longmans, Green, 1955.

Keats. 4th ed. rev. and enlarged. London: Cape, 1955. New York: Noonday Press, 1955.

Unprofessional Essays. London: Cape, 1956. Fair Lawn, N.J.: Essential Books, 1956.

Love, Freedom and Society. London: Cape, 1957.

Selected Bibliography

Katherine Mansfield and Other Literary Studies. Foreword by T. S. ELIOT. London: Constable, 1959. Chester Springs, Pa.: Dufour Editions, 1960.

Not as the Scribes. Ed. with intr. by ALEC R. VIDLER. London: S.C.M. Press, 1959. New York: Horizon Press, 1959

Selected Criticism. Chosen and intr. by RICHARD REES. London: Oxford University Press, 1960.*

* A second selection of Murry's essays, also edited by Richard Rees, is due for publication by the Southern Illinois University Press, Carbondale, Illinois, in the Spring of 1969.

2. Uncollected Works

The books listed above include the more important of Murry's many essays and reviews, although some of his later uncollected ones, especially those published in *The Aryan Path* and *The London Magazine,* are of interest. A selection is given below.

Published in *The Aryan Path*:

"Western Mysticism," I, 2 (February, 1930), 83-88.
"The Purgation of Suffering," I, 10 (October, 1930), 648-51.
"The Doctrine of Will in Shakespeare," IV, 7 (July, 1933), 479-83.
"Professors and Poets," VI, 7 (July, 1935), 446-50.
"The Value of Poetry in the Social Order," XI, 9 (September, 1940), 439-42.

Published in *The London Magazine*:

Review of *The Fire and the Fountain: An Essay on Poetry* by JOHN PRESS, II, 11 (November, 1955), 79-82.
"The Living Dead—I: D. H. Lawrence," III, 5 (May, 1956), 57-63.
"Coming to London—VIII," III, 7 (July, 1956), 30-37. Review of *The Craft of Letters in England* ed. JOHN LEHMANN, III, 12 (December, 1956), 69-75.
Review of *Form and Meaning in Drama* by H. D. F. KITTO and *The Harvest of Tragedy* by T. R. HENN, IV, 3 (March, 1957), 61-63.
Review of *The Lion and the Honeycomb* by R. P. BLACKMUR and *The Man of Letters in the Modern World* by ALLEN TATE, IV, 5 (May, 1957), 66-69.

SECONDARY SOURCES

BEER, J. B. "John Middleton Murry," *Critical Quarterly,* III, 1 (Spring, 1961), 59-66. A perceptive review article assessing Murray's achievement as critic.

CRÉPIN, ANDRÉ. "John Middleton Murry et le sens allégorique de la vie," *Études Anglaises*, XIV, 4 (Oct.-Dec., 1961), 321-30. A general survey, though with some emphasis on Murry's view of life as "a continual allegory."

GIRARD, DENIS. "John Middleton Murry, D. H. Lawrence et Albert Schweitzer," *Études Anglaises*, XII, 3 (July-Sept., 1959), 212-21. A comparative summary of the three attitudes to social and spiritual values.

HEATH, WILLIAM W. "The Literary Criticism of John Middleton Murry," *Publications of the Modern Language Association*, LXX, 1 (March, 1955), 47-57. Particularly concerned with Murry's critical principles and method.

HEPPENSTALL, RAYNER. *John Middleton Murry: A Study in Excellent Normality*. London: Cape, 1934. An early but still helpful appreciation of Murry.

———. *Four Absentees*. London: Barrie and Rockliff, 1960. Personal reminiscences of Murry, one of the "four absentees."

JONES, JOHN. "Murry Revaluated," *The New Statesman*, December 12, 1959, p. 848. Review article giving a judicious estimate of Murry as critic.

KAUFMANN, R. J. "On Using an Obsessed Critic: John Middleton Murry," *The Graduate Student of English*, III, 2 (Winter, 1960), 4-8. Distinguishes Murry from the "professional" critic.

KNIGHT, G. WILSON. "J. Middleton Murry." *Of Books and Humankind*. Ed. John Butt. London: Routledge and Kegan Paul, 1964. Emphasizes effect of Murry's mystical experience on his criticism.

LAWRENCE, D. H. *The Collected Letters of D. H. Lawrence*. 2 vols. Ed. Harry T. Moore. New York: Viking Press, 1962.

LAWRENCE, FRIEDA. *Frieda Lawrence: The Memoirs and Correspondence*. Ed. E. W. Tedlock. London: Heinemann, 1961.

LEA, F. A. *The Life of John Middleton Murry*. London: Methuen, 1959. The official biography; indispensable to a study of Murry.

MAIRET, PHILIP. *John Middleton Murry*. Published for The British Council and the National Book League. London: Longmans, Green, 1958. Excellent introduction to Murry's literary criticism.

MANSFIELD, KATHERINE. *Journal of Katherine Mansfield*. Ed. John Middleton Murry. London: Constable, 1927. Definitive edition, London: Constable, 1954.

———. *The Letters of Katherine Mansfield*. 2 vols. Ed. John Middleton Murry. London: Constable, 1928.

———. *Katherine Mansfield's Letters to John Middleton Murry 1913-1922*. Ed. John Middleton Murry. London: Constable, 1951.

———. *The Scrapbook of Katherine Mansfield*. Ed. John Middleton Murry. London: Constable, 1939.

Selected Bibliography

MILLER, KARL. "The Murry-Go-Round," *The Spectator,* January 8, 1960, p. 44. Review article emphasizing Murry's positive contribution to the maintenance of literary values.

MURRY, MARY MIDDLETON. *To Keep Faith.* London: Constable, 1959. Personal memoir.

READ, HERBERT. Review of *The Life of John Middleton Murry* by F. A. Lea, *To Keep Faith* by Mary Middleton Murry, and *Katherine Mansfield and Other Literary Studies* by J. Middleton Murry. *The London Magazine,* VII, 1 (January, 1960), 64-67. A review article offering a sensitive evaluation of Murry's literary significance.

REES, RICHARD. *A Theory of My Time.* London: Secker and Warburg, 1963. Contains many reminiscences of Murry and an appreciation of his "intellectual eminence."

SEAVER, GEORGE. *Albert Schweitzer: A Vindication—Being a Reply to "The Challenge of Schweitzer" by John Middleton Murry.* London: James Clarke, 1950.

STANFORD, DEREK. "Middleton Murry as Literary Critic," *Essays in Criticism.* VIII, 1 (January, 1958), 60-67. A brief survey of Murry as a primarily Romantic critic.

WATSON, J. H. "A Good Workman and His Friends: Recollections of John Middleton Murry," *The London Magazine,* VI, 5 (May, 1959), 51-55. Emphasizes the appeal of Murry as craftsman and critic to "labouring folk."

In addition to the above, works on D. H. Lawrence and Katherine Mansfield frequently contain many references to Murry. The following in particular should be noted.

ALDINGTON, RICHARD. *Portrait of a Genius But . . . .* London: Heinemann, 1950.

ALPERS, ANTONY. *Katherine Mansfield, A Biography.* New York: Knopf, 1953.

CARSWELL, CATHERINE. *The Savage Pilgrimage.* Rev. ed. London: Secker, 1932.

DALY, SARALYN R. *Katherine Mansfield.* New York: Twayne Publishers, 1965.

MOORE, HARRY T. *The Intelligent Heart: The Story of D. H. Lawrence.* New York: Farrar, Straus and Young, 1954.

NEHLS, EDWARD. *D. H. Lawrence, A Composite Biography.* 3 vols. Madison: University of Wisconsin Press, 1957-1959.

Index

Family background and education at Christ's Hospital and Oxford, 23-25; love of English countryside, experience in Paris, early editorial experience, meeting with Katherine Mansfield and D. H. Lawrence, 25-27; marriages, experience of two world wars, general development, 27-30; experiments with poetry, fiction and drama, 30-33; influence of "the Russian Soul," critical study of Dostoevsky, 33-39; Classical training and mystical experience as elements in criticism, 40-43; outstanding editorial work, running debate on Classicism and Romanticism